Poems 2
Teacher's Book

edited by

Michael Harrison
Christopher Stuart-Clark

Oxford University Press 1980

ISBN 0 19 834269 1

Set, printed and bound in Great Britain by
Fakenham Press Limited, Fakenham, Norfolk

Contents

Introduction iv
Ways into a poem vi
How to use this book viii
Techniques in poetry x
Bibliography xiv
Themes xvi
Contents of anthology 3
Anthology 6–125
Teacher's notes 126
Index of titles and first lines 205
Index of authors 207
Acknowledgements 208

The publishers would like to thank the following people for permission to reproduce copyright material:

Animal Graphics for 26; Ardea for 31; Arctic Camera for 100–101; Janet and Colin Bord for 18–21, 28; British Rail (Western Region) for 48–49; British Tourist Authority for 32, 80; Maurice Carroll for 108; CEGB for 67; COI for 86–87 (Crown Copyright); Commonwealth War Graves Commission for 82–83; Hunter Cordaiy for 14–15, 42–43, 120; the Dean and Chapter of Ely Cathedral for 44; Nick Fogden for 10–11, 16–17, 36, 58, 61, 78, 90–91, 114; Fay Godwin for 107, 112, 115; Greater London Council for 104; Sue Heap for 29, 56; ITN for 12–13; Lawrence Lawry for 88, 92–93; Barry Lewis for 33, 62, 64, 68–69, 71, 96–97; Nick Lyons for 44; Maurice Nimmo for 52–53, 55; Oxford Mail for 75; Press Association for 103; Mrs Amoret Scott for 8–9; John Topham Picture Library for 34–35; Simon Warner for 46–47, 76, 94–95; Rita Winstanley for 37, 66.

The publishers would also like to thank Mrs L. Holmes and Relko for their kind assistance with some photographs.

Introduction

'What the child, and the child-in-the-adult, most enjoys in poetry . . . is the manipulation of language for its own sake, the sound and rhythm of words.' W. H. Auden, Introduction to *A Choice of de la Mare's Verse* (Faber, 1963)

'We can sum up by saying that whatever else the pupil takes away from his experience of literature in school he should have learned to see it as a source of pleasure, as something that will continue to be part of his life.' Bullock Report, *A Language for Life* (HMSO, 1975)

'Everyone is a poet who can dance in time to a band at a party or march in step on parade. Poetry is the shortest way of saying things. It also looks nicer on the page than prose. It gives room to think and dream.' Sir John Betjeman, *The New Dragon Book of Verse* (OUP, 1977)

Poems 2 is the second book in a poetry teaching course. The course hopes to develop an enjoyment that will last. We believe that to enjoy poetry you have to understand something of how it works. In *Poems* we led from poetry that children had met already, such as jokes, riddles, and playground rhymes, through simple poems to a stage 'where the reader needs to work at a poem.'

In *Poems 2* we start with limericks and short epitaphs, both forms which children are likely to have met already, and move through some simple poems by well-known modern poets to some more advanced poems by modern and earlier established English poets. Thus we hope to give an insight into the main body of English poetry.

The use of poetry from earlier generations in *Poems 2* raises three problems:

1 The language is unfamiliar and therefore difficult;
2 There may be references to past events of which we are now ignorant or to a formerly commonly-known culture which may now be a closed book to our pupils;
3 The expectations and sensitivities of previous generations were quite different. Reading the love poetry of earlier centuries, for example, may give the modern adolescent the impression that poets talk about it a lot but do nothing.

These three problems can make these earlier poems seem irrelevant and unappealing. We hope that the arrangement of *Poems 2* may encourage children to suspend their judgment long enough to give the poems a chance. By this stage the reader should be convinced that poetry is on his side. Simple fun should give way to subtler, more lasting pleasures – but the pleasures must be there.

The Teacher's Book provides four ways into a poem. Children who have worked through the course will gradually have acquired a routine that will help them approach a poem. In *Poems 2* we signpost one of these ways for each poem.

Ways into a poem

Story: What is the poem about?
Some poems tell simple incidents and others tell full stories. Poems can be 'about' a huge variety of subjects. In *Poems 2* we use this signpost for poems that tell a fairly straightforward story.

Feeling: What feelings does the poem evoke in us?
Poems are used to explore and to record feelings such as excitement, terror, joy, love, happiness. The feelings themselves can be considered separately from the way in which they are evoked.

Pattern: How are the words of the poem arranged?
In poems, as in other art forms, we look for some regularity or repetition. It can come from rhyme, rhythm, or the shape of the words on the page.

Image: What pictures does the poem create in our minds?
In *Poems 2* descriptive poems and examples of simile and metaphor show the visual and aural presentation of imagery.

In the notes on the poems, we pick out and concentrate on one or two of these ways. But the other ways are always relevant; sometimes we draw attention to these in the work we have suggested.

A Teacher's page is in four sections:

Section 1 has comments for the teacher about the poem: it explains why the poem is included where it is and highlights which of the four approaches is intended as the main one. The language in this section is geared to the teacher.

Section 2 consists of questions for the class. Some or all of these may be used for discussion or as the basis for written answers. The language in this section is geared to the child.

Section 3, where it appears, contains comments on the rhyme and rhythm/metre of the poem and/or on the figurative language used; this is in language geared to the teacher. It may also include some questions on these technical sides to the poetry, in language geared to the child. These questions are printed in italics, and the section is marked off on the page by heavy rules.

Section 4 contains follow-up work, with cross-references to other poems in the book and to other anthologies (*V* = *Voices*; *NDBV* = *New Dragon Book of Verse*).

All the anthologies mentioned are available in paper-back. The three volumes of *Voices* are referred to regularly: these are, we feel, books which all children should have the opportunity to meet.

The teacher's material concentrates on the content and structure of the particular poem. Only in a few cases have we used the poem as a stimulus for the children's own writing; this we call the 'centrifugal' approach to contrast it with the 'centripetal' emphasis on the text of the poem. The poems may, of course, all be used as a stimulus for writing, art, or drama, but it is much more important that they are enjoyed for themselves.

We want to stress that pupils will certainly benefit simply by reading through a poem and enjoying it. Sometimes there is no need to do anything else. To work through the book from cover to cover, using all the teacher's material, would be monotonous. We hope that the teacher will be flexible and selective in the use he makes of our comments, questions, cross-references, and follow-up poems.

How to use this book

A suggested lesson pattern: READ DISCUSS READ

The teacher reads the poem while the pupils have the anthology either open or shut. You may want to read it more than once or, occasionally, to get a pupil to read it.

Read out the first question for class discussion (see second paragraph opposite). Move on to the next question when it seems right.

Finally, either the teacher or pupils (or both) read the poem again.

Some of the follow-up work on the opposite page can be used.

Three variations

1 Instead of having class discussion, split up for group discussion.

The groups can report back.

End with each group, or some of the groups, reading to the class.

2 The questions can be used for written answers by being read out, written on the blackboard, or reproduced. This can be a preliminary to discussion.

3 We repeat: please don't stick to the same lesson format to the point of boredom. Have some lessons that are just reading poems for pure enjoyment.

We believe there are two very important points about teaching poetry:

All poetry is written primarily to be heard. We hope that any introduction to a poem will start with the teacher reading the poem to the class or playing the cassette, where relevant. The teacher may choose whether to make any preliminary remarks before reading and whether to have the class following in the book or not. Many of the poems have an element of surprise in them. You can keep this sense of surprise by letting the pupils hear the poem first, and see it later. A class discussion can then follow, along the lines suggested in 'How to use this Book'. After the discussion the class should read the poem aloud, either in groups or individually. The pupils should now be able to comprehend the poem more fully and should read the poem aloud with more understanding.

In all discussion on a poem it is important to lead back into the poem. There is a natural 'centrifugal' tendency to talk about one's own experience at the expense of the poem. Keep asking for supporting evidence *from the text of the poem itself.*

Follow-up work

Note: Some of this section is what we have described as **centrifugal**: leading away from the poem. These activities will normally follow the suggested lesson although, for variation's sake, they will sometimes form the complete lesson.

1 Use the poem as a starting-point for pupil's writing.
2 Ask the pupils to collect poems that will go with the lesson poem in some way.
3 Over the year pupils can make a personal anthology of poems and lines from poems that they like. These can be illustrated.
4 Pupils can be encouraged to learn by heart poems and lines from poems that they like.
5 Pupils present their anthologies to the class, individually or in groups. These can be read out, written and displayed, or tape-recorded.
6 Some poems will lead naturally into drama.
7 At the end of term, or of the year, hold a request programme of favourite poems.
8 Make full use of BBC broadcasts to add variety and stimulus, especially *Living Language* and *Listening and Writing*.

Themes

We have provided a list of themes (p. xvi) for those who wish to integrate poetry into topic work, rather than to follow this book through from the beginning to the end. The relevant teacher's pages will lead to similar poems in *Voices.* For further poems see Morris: *Where's That Poem?* (Basil Blackwell).

Techniques in poetry

Some classes will be ready for a more technical approach to poetry. On some pages we have added a further section (**Section 3**) which can be used at the teacher's discretion. In *Poems 2* we introduce three main areas to explore:

1 Foregrounding: the use of the unexpected and unusual.
2 Patterning: the use of rhythm and rhyme.
3 Word-play: figurative language and honest deceptions.

1 Foregrounding

Works of art deviate in some way from the established, expected pattern. This deviation catches our attention, like a figure in the foreground of a picture. It is this deviation, or foregrounding, that we concentrate on when studying any work of art. Jokes rely on the same technique as in the limerick ending *I always try to get as many words into the last line as I possibly can.*

Note that the deviation can be towards unusual regularity (e.g. constant rhyme, an unwanted, even embarrassing, feature of speech or prose) as well as towards strangeness and originality.

Sections on Foregrounding will be found on pages 127, 134 and 140.

2 Patterning

In the Teacher's Book to *Poems* we encouraged some attention to the pattern of a poem to bring some awareness of the poem's construction. In *Poems 2* we develop the idea of pattern to include recognition of rhyme and of rhythm or metre.

It is possible to 'kill' a poem quickly by treating it as a series of lines, sounds and syllables to be analysed and fitted to a formula. But some understanding of rhyme and metre should help children to appreciate the construction of a poem and to admire the 'art which conceals the art'. So we have included some questions, separate from those on the text of the poem, which will bring out recognition of rhyme schemes and an understanding of basic metre. Some children will be fascinated by dissection into metre, others will not be attracted at all. The teacher must judge whether the class is ready to use the material.

A rhyme scheme is easy to recognize, where it exists. The study of rhythm and metre can be more complicated. It may be enough to count the beats in a line and recognize, for example, the four beats in

> Nóise of hámmers ónce I heárd

But it may be profitable to go on to find the basic metrical foot

(iamb: ˘ ´; trochee ´ ˘; dactyl ´ ˘ ˘; anapaest ˘ ˘ ´)

and describe the lines as trimeters, tetrameters, pentameters. To give some examples:

> Thĕn Goó|dy̆, whó|hăd nó|thĭng sáid,
> Hĕr bún|dlĕ fróm|hĕr láp|lĕt fáll;
> Ănd knéel|ĭng ón|thĕ stícks|, shĕ práyed
> Tŏ Gód|thăt ís|thĕ júdge|ŏf áll

may be said to have four beats to a line or may be said to be in 'iambic tetrameters'.

> Nóise ŏf |hámmĕrs|ónce Ĭ|heárd,
> Mány̆|hámmĕrs,|búsy̆|hámmĕrs,
> Béatĭng|, shápĭng|, níght ănd |dáy,
> Shápĭng,|béatĭng|dúst ănd |cláy

has four beats to the line and is in 'trochaic tetrameters'.

> Whĕn ă mán|hăth nŏ frée|dŏm tŏ fíght|fŏr ăt hóme
> Lĕt hĭm cóm|băt fŏr thát|ŏf hĭs néigh|bŏurs;
> Lĕt hĭm thínk|ŏf thĕ glór|ĭes ŏf Gréece|ănd ŏf Róme
> Ănd gĕt knócked |ŏn thĕ héad |fŏr hĭs láb|ŏurs

has four/three beats to a line and is in 'anapaestic tetrameters/trimeters'; alternately.

> Whó ĭs thăt|chíld Ĭ sēe|wándĕrĭng|, wándĕrĭng
> Dówn by̆ thĕ|síde ŏf thĕ|quívĕrĭng|stréam?
> Whý dŏes hĕ|séem nŏt tŏ|héar, thoŭgh Ĭ|cáll tŏ hĭm?
> Whére dŏes hĕ|cóme frŏm, ănd |whát ĭs hĭs|náme?

has four/three beats to the line and is in 'dactylic tetrameters/trimeters', alternately.

3 Figurative language:

i This is best seen as part of a continuum:

literal ⟵————————————⟶ figurative
language

rather than as a water-tight compartment. Much of everyday language consists of dead or dying metaphors, and there is a natural ambiguity in words that we need a context to decipher.

ii Simile and metaphor

A simile is often thought of as a second-class metaphor but they both have their virtues and their places. While metaphor is more concise and immediate, simile can be unambiguous by specifying the ground of the comparison. In what could be the most famous first line in English poetry:

'I wandered lonely as a cloud'

the use of a simile makes it quite clear exactly what attribute of clouds is relevant here; obviously most of their other attributes would hardly apply, even metaphorically, to Wordsworth. Metaphors tend to make concrete and explicit what is abstract and elusive in human experience. A common form of metaphor is **personification** where an abstraction is figuratively represented as a human: the wind wailed.

A section on Similes will be found on pages 134 and 135.

Sections on Dead Metaphors will be found on pages 129 and 142.

Sections on Metaphors will be found on pages 140, 157 and 184.

A section on Personification will be found on page 141.

A revision section on figurative language will be found on pages 145 and 146.

iii Honest deceptions

This is Geoffrey Leech's phrase for three ways of deliberately masking the truth without the intention of hiding it. He explains, 'If you dress up as a rabbit at a fancy-dress ball, you do not intend to be mistaken for a rabbit.'[1] The three ways are:
(a) Exaggeration (hyperbole)
(b) Understatement (litotes)
(c) Irony

Sections on Exaggeration will be found on pages 136, 138 and 161.

Sections on Understatement will be found on pages 167, 175 and 192.

Sections on Irony will be found on pages 137 and 165.

[1] Geoffrey N. Leech: *A Linguistic Guide To English Poetry* (Longman).

Bibliography

1 Books on teaching poetry

Douglas Barnes: *From Communication to Curriculum* (Penguin)
An essential examination of the problems of discussion in class.
Geoffrey N. Leech: *A Linguistic Guide to English Poetry* (Longman)
The best guide to techniques in poetry.
Michael Marland: *The Craft of the Classroom* (Heinemann Educational)
Covers the practical problems thoroughly and sensibly.
I. A. Richards: *Practical Criticism* (Routledge and Kegan Paul)
Examines the difficulties in talking about poetry, with some suggestions for practice.
Frank Whitehead: *The Disappearing Dais* (Chatto and Windus)
Useful advice on the 'centripetal' approach.

2 An invaluable reference book

Helen Morris: *Where's That Poem?* (Basil Blackwell)
Lists of poems arranged by themes.

3 Some relevant hardback poetry books for the teacher

Charles Causley: *Collected Poems* (Macmillan)
Ted Hughes: *Moon-Bells and Other Poems* (Chatto and Windus)
The Earth-Owl (Faber and Faber)
Season Songs (Faber and Faber)
Barbara Ireson: *Moving Along* (Evans)
Roger McGough & Michael Rosen: *You Tell Me* (Kestrel)
Gareth Owen: *Salford Road* (Kestrel)
Michael Rosen: *Wouldn't You Like to Know* (André Deutsch)

4 Books for the class library, all paperbacks

Hilaire Belloc: *Selected Cautionary Verses* (Puffin)
Charles Causley: *The Puffin Book of Magic Verse*
Charles Causley: *The Puffin Book of Salt-Sea Verse* (Puffin)
Charles Causley: *Figgie Hobbin* (Puffin)
David Davis: *A Single Star* (Puffin)
Eleanor Graham: *A Puffin Quartet of Poets* (Puffin)

Michael Harrison and Christopher Stuart-Clark: *The New Dragon Book of Verse* (OUP)
Ted Hughes: *Meet My Folks* (Puffin)
David Jackson: *Ways of Talking* (Ward Lock Educational)
Michael Rosen: *Mind Your Own Business* (Armada Lion)
Michael Rosen: *The Bakerloo Flea* (Longman Knock-Out)
Dennis Saunders: *Hist Whist* (Piccolo)
Dennis Saunders and Vincent Oliver: *Poems and Pictures* series (Evans)
Ian Serraillier: *I'll Tell You a Tale* (Puffin)
Geoffrey Summerfield: *Voices 1 to 111* (Penguin)
Julia Watson: *A Children's Zoo* (Armada)
Kaye Webb: *I Like This Poem* (Puffin)
Raymond Wilson: *Time's Delights* (Beaver)
Kit Wright: *Rabbiting On and Other Poems* (Fontana Lions)

Themes

Animals
Glasgow October 1972 26
Milk for the Cat 27
The Galloping Cat 24
Fetching Cows 30
The Dog Lovers 72
My Mother saw a Dancing Bear 73
Song of the Battery Hen 74
Pegasus 123

Birds
A Widow Bird 29
Once at Piertarvit 68
Numbers 71
Song 70
A Dream 90
The Prince of Love 89

Cats
26–27

Children/Childhood
Saturdays I put on my boots to go wading 22
Child on top of a Greenhouse 33
The Carol of the Poor Children 41
Midnight on the Great Western 50
Thistle (Lee) 54
Who? 103
Schoolmistress 105
An Elementary School Classroom in a Slum 106

Death
Epitaphs 8
Song 43
Requiem 45
An Inscription by the Sea 45
The Spiritual Railway 44
Here lies a poor woman 45
On moonlit heath 115
The Hangman at Home 114
Rizpah 116
Simplify Me 125

Fables
Advice to a Knight 16
Goody Blake and Harry Gill 18
Icarus Allsorts 86
You'd better believe him 108
Good Taste 109
The Future 113

Fantasy
The Forlorn Sea 14
Advice to a Knight 16
The Galloping Cat 24
from *The Prelude* 76
You'd better believe him 108
Good Taste 109

Fear
Haunted 120

Now the hungry lion roars 122

Flowers
Daysies 34
The Lily 36
The Dandelion's pallid tube 37
The fear of flowers 52

Fog
38–39

Jokes
Limericks 6
Short Epitaphs 8
I went to the doctor, yes 10
Here is the news 12
Think of this tower-block 59

Love
88–97

Night
Corner Seat 51
November Night, Edinburgh 39
Meeting at Night 88
The Witches' Charm 122

Old Age
Goody Blake and Harry Gill 18
Evans 98
Upstream 100
The Qualification 113
The Future 113
Rizpah 116

People
Limericks 6
Epitaphs 8
Advice to a Knight 16
Epitaph in Lydford 42
Goody Blake and Harry Gill 18
A Red, Red Rose 91
The Passionate Shepherd 94
To His Coy Mistress 96
Evans 98
Plastic Woman 99
The Astigmatic 102
Schoolmistress 105
The Hangman at Home 114
Who? 103
Man in the Bowler Hat 124

Revenge
Goody Blake and Harry Gill 18
Thistles (Hughes) 56
Slough 64

School
105–106

Songs
Friday Morning 40
The Carol of the Poor Children 41
Harp Song of the Dane Women 79
The War Song of Dinas Vawr 82
On the Massacre of Glencoe 84
Song 43

Stories
The Forlorn Sea 14
Goody Blake and Harry Gill 18
Saturdays I put on my boots to go wading 22
Once at Piertarvit 68
You'd better believe him 108
Good Taste 109
A Brown Paper Carrier Bag 110
Rizpah 116
Pegasus 123
Icarus Allsorts 86
The War Song of Dinas Vawr 82
On the Late Massacre in Piedmont 83
On the Massacre of Glencoe 84

Surroundings
November Night, Edinburgh 39
Think of this tower-block 59
Slough 64
The Hammers 63
Number 14 63
Telegraph Poles 66
The Pylons 67
from *The Prelude* 77
Abbey Tomb 80
Meeting at Night 88
Lines 93
Evans 98
Upstream 100
An Elementary School Classroom in a Slum 106
Haunted 120

Thistles
52–57

Trains
46–51
The Spiritual Railway 44

Vikings
Thistles (Hughes) 56
Harp Song of the Dane Women 79
Abbey Tomb 80

War
78–87

Wind
The Wind Begun 32
Child on Top of a Greenhouse 33

Winter
November Night, Edinburgh 39
The Carol of the Poor Children 41

Wordplay
I went to the doctor, yes 10
The Qualification 113

Contents

□ Indicates that the poem is recorded on the cassette (isbn 019 840315·1)
□□ Recorded by the poet himself

Limericks 6
Epitaphs 8
I went to the doctor, yes *Michael Rosen* 10
□□ Here is the News *Michael Rosen* 12
The Forlorn Sea *Stevie Smith* 14
Advice to a Knight *T. H. Jones* 16
Old English Riddle *Kevin Crossley-Holland* 17
□ Goody Blake and Harry Gill *William Wordsworth* 18
□□ Saturdays I put on my boots *Michael Rosen* 22
□□ The Galloping Cat *Stevie Smith* 24
Glasgow October 1972 *Edwin Morgan* 26
Milk for the Cat *Harold Monro* 27
A Widow Bird *Percy Bysshe Shelley* 29
Fetching Cows *Norman MacCaig* 30
The Spider holds a Silver Ball *Emily Dickinson* 31
The Wind begun to rock the Grass *Emily Dickinson* 32
Child on Top of a Greenhouse *Theodore Roethke* 33
Daysies *Geoffrey Chaucer* 34
The Lily *William Blake* 36
The Dandelion's pallid tube *Emily Dickinson* 37
Mist in the Meadows *John Clare* 37
The Fog *W. H. Davies* 38
The fog comes *Carl Sandburg* 39
November Night, Edinburgh *Norman MacCaig* 39
Friday Morning *Sydney Carter* 40
The Carol of the Poor Children *Richard Middleton* 41
Epitaph in Lydford Churchyard 42
Song *Christina Rossetti* 43
The Spiritual Railway 44
Requiem *Robert Louis Stevenson* 45
Here lies a poor woman 45
An Inscription by the Sea 45
The Express *Stephen Spender* 46
A Local Train of Thought *Siegfried Sassoon* 47
Tremors *Stewart Conn* 48
Midnight on the Great Western *Thomas Hardy* 50
Corner Seat *Louis MacNeice* 51

To a Fat Lady Seen from the Train *Frances Cornford* 51
□ The Fear of Flowers *John Clare* 52
□ Thistledown *Andrew Young* 53
□□ Thistle *Laurie Lee* 54
□□ Thistles *Ted Hughes* 56
□□ Thistles *Jon Stallworthy* 57
□□ Think of this tower-block *Michael Rosen* 59
The Hammers *Ralph Hodgson* 63
Number 14 *Keith Bosley* 63
Slough *John Betjeman* 64
Telegraph Poles *Paul Dehn* 66
The Pylons *Stephen Spender* 67
Once at Piertarvit *Alastair Reid* 68
Song *John Keats* 70
Numbers *Stevie Smith* 71
The Dog Lovers *Spike Milligan* 72
My Mother saw a Dancing Bear *Charles Causley* 73
Song of the Battery Hen *Edwin Brock* 74
Prelude, from The *William Wordsworth* 76
Stanzas *Lord Byron* 78
□ Harp Song of the Dane Women *Rudyard Kipling* 79
Abbey Tomb *Patricia Beer* 80
The War Song of Dinas Vawr *Thomas Love Peacock* 82
□ On the Late Massacre in Piedmont *John Milton* 83
On the Massacre of Glencoe *Sir Walter Scott* 84
Oh stay at home, my lad, and plough *A. E. Housman* 85
□□ Icarus Allsorts *Roger McGough* 86
Meeting at Night *Robert Browning* 88
My mistress' eyes are nothing like the sun *William Shakespeare* 89
□ The Prince of Love *William Blake* 89
A Dream *Christina Rossetti* 90
A Red, Red Rose *Robert Burns* 91
First Love *John Clare* 92
Lines *Percy Bysshe Shelley* 93
□ The Passionate Shepherd to his Love *Christopher Marlowe* 94
□ Come Live with Me *David Campbell* 95
To His Coy Mistress *Andrew Marvell* 96
Evans *R. S. Thomas* 98
Plastic Woman *Spike Milligan* 99
Upstream *Ikinilik* 100
The Astigmatic *Philip Hobsbaum* 102
Who? *Charles Causley* 103
Schoolmistress (Miss Humm) *Clive Sansom* 105
An Elementary School Class Room in a Slum *Stephen Spender* 106

□□ You'd better believe him *Brian Patten* 108
Good Taste *Christopher Logue* 109
There is no Frigate like a Book *Emily Dickinson* 109
A Brown Paper Carrierbag *Roger McGough* 110
New Members Welcome *Spike Milligan* 111
The Qualification *Tom Leonard* 113
The Future *Spike Milligan* 113
The Hangman at Home *Carl Sandburg* 114
On moonlit heath and lonesome bank *A. E. Housman* 115
□ Rizpah *Alfred, Lord Tennyson* 116
Haunted *Siegfried Sassoon* 120
Now the hungry lion roars *William Shakespeare* 122
The Witches' Charm *Ben Jonson* 122
Pegasus *Eleanor Farjeon* 123
The Man in the Bowler Hat *A. S. J. Tessimond* 124
Simplify me when I'm Dead *Keith Douglas* 125

There was a young man from Bengal
Who went to a fancy dress ball;
He thought he would risk it
And go as a biscuit,
But a dog ate him up in the hall.

A man on the flying trapeze
Emitted a terrible sneeze.
The consequent force
Shot him right off his course,
And they found him next day in some trees.

'Open wide,' said a dentist called Bert
To a man-eating shark whose teeth hurt.
'When I've finished the drilling
I'll give you a filling.'
He did – and the filling was Bert.

Said a buffalo hunter in Streatham,
'There are buffaloes here and I'll get 'em.
There's no need to fret
If you've not seen 'em yet –
They're around, but you've simply not met 'em.'

There was a young lady from Ryde
Who ate a green apple and died;
The apple fermented
Inside the lamented,
And made cider inside her inside.

There was an old man from Nantucket
Who kept all his cash in a bucket.
His daughter, named Nan,
Ran away with a man,
And as for the bucket, Nan tucket.

There once was a girl, Laura Norder,
Went out with Bill Posters, who bored 'er.
They met Eva Brick—
She'd been in the nick,
But her boyfriend, Van Dal, still adored 'er.

There was a young man of Japan
Who wrote verse that never would scan.
When they said 'But the thing
Doesn't go with a swing,'
He said, 'Yes, but I always like to get as many words into the last line as I possibly can.'

On Leslie Moore
Here lies what's left
Of Leslie Moore.
No Les
No more.
On Sir John Guise
Here lies the body of Sir John Guise,
Nobody laughs and nobody cries;
Where his soul is, and how it fares,
Nobody knows and nobody cares.
On Dr. Chard
Here lies the corpse of Doctor Chard,
Who'd fill'd half of this churchyard.

On a Dentist

Stranger, approach this spot with gravity;
John Brown is filling his last cavity.

On a Man Named Merideth

Here lies one blown out of breath,
Who lived a merry life, and died a Merideth.

On a Liar

Even my tombstone gives the truth away,
It says to all who face this little hill
'Hic iacet': 'Here I lie'. Or should it say
Here I lie – still?

On John Ford's Wife

Here lies Mary – the wife of John Ford.
We hope her soul is gone to the Lord.
But if for Hell she has changed this life,
She had better be there than John Ford's wife.

On a 'Shrew'

Here lies my poor wife, much lamented,
She is happy and I am contented.

Midland Epitaph

'Er as was 'as gone from me.
Us and is 'll go ter she.

Here lies I, no wonder I'm dead,
For a broad-wheel'd waggon went over my head.

On Sir John Vanbrugh (The Architect)

Under this stone, Reader, survey
Dead Sir John Vanbrugh's house of clay.
Lie heavy on him, Earth! For he
Laid many heavy loads on thee!

I went to the doctor, yes,
I went to him
and I said – 'Doctor, Doctor,
it's Roads,' I said. 'Roads?' he says.
'Roads,' I said.
'No such thing,' he says.
'I've got Roads, Doctor,
very bad Roads.
I've got long distance lorryworry
one way only lorryworry.
They say:
No U-turns Ahead.
I know I turned my head,
but I saw a zebra crossing
and a bus eating a traffic jam.
I can hear
unhappy new gears.
When traffic's light
at traffic lights
I see red
amber
red and amber
red already.

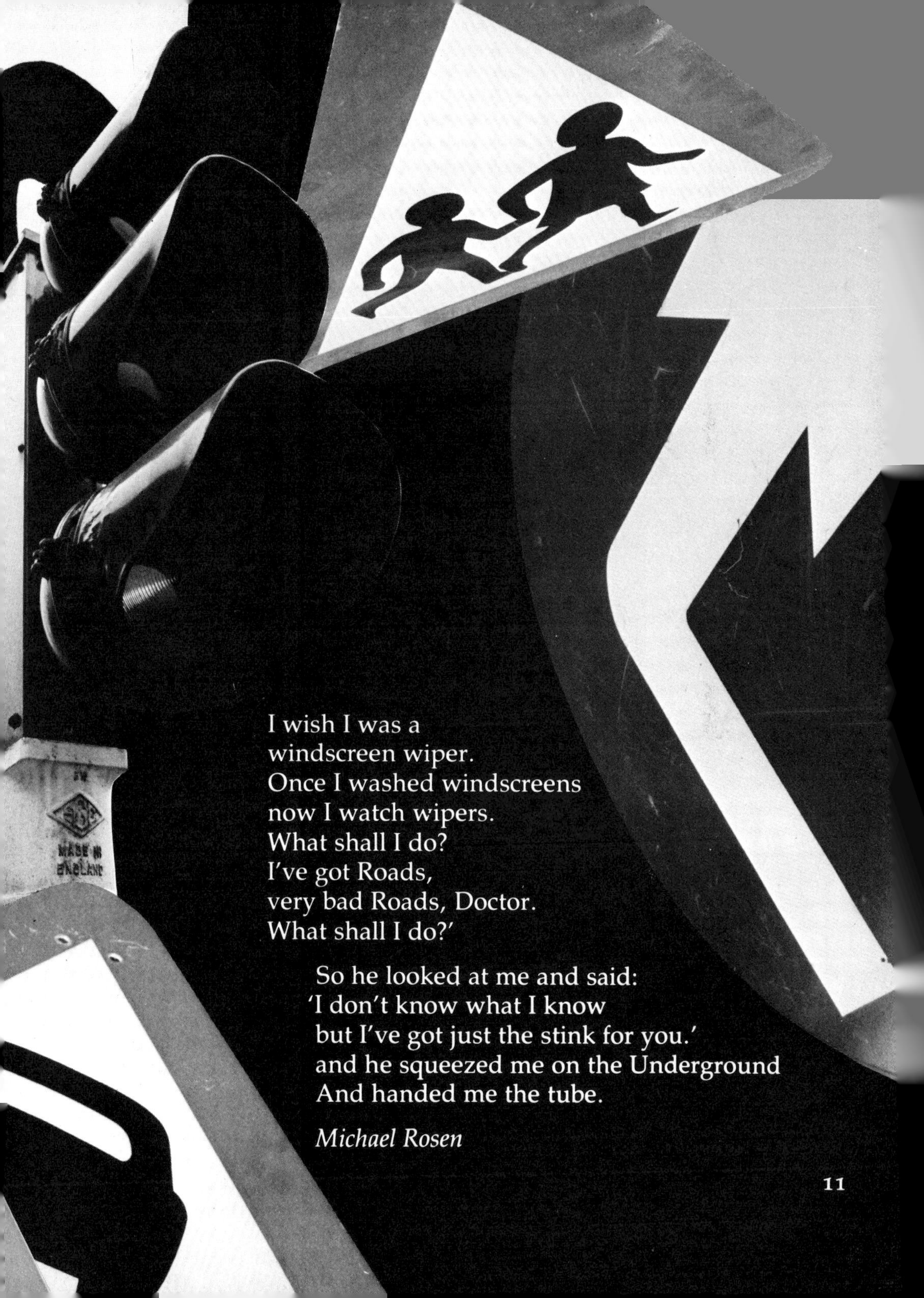

I wish I was a
windscreen wiper.
Once I washed windscreens
now I watch wipers.
What shall I do?
I've got Roads,
very bad Roads, Doctor.
What shall I do?'

So he looked at me and said:
'I don't know what I know
but I've got just the stink for you.'
and he squeezed me on the Underground
And handed me the tube.

Michael Rosen

Here is the News:

In Manchester today a man was seen
with hair on top of his head.
Over now straightway to our Northern correspondent:
Hugh Snews.

'It's been a really incredible day
here in Manchester. Scenes like this
have been seen here everyday
for years and years. It's now quite certain
no one will be saying anything about this
for months to come. One eyewitness said so.
"Are you sure?" I said.
She said: "No."
Back to you in London.'

All round the world,
newspapers, radio and television
have taken no notice of this story
and already a Prime Minister
has said nothing about it at all.
What next?
Rumour McRumourbungle,
Expert expert in expert experts?

'I doubt it. I doubt whether
anyone *will* doubt it – but I do.'

'What?'

'Doubt it.'

Thank you, Rumour McRumourbungle.
But how did it all begin?
As dawn broke in Manchester it soon became clear.
It's quite likely there was a lot of air in the air.
An hour after a few minutes had gone,
a couple of seconds passed
and a minute later at 12.15
it was a quarter past twelve.
Suddenly from across the other side of the road,
on the side facing this side,
there was the same road from the other side.
This side was now facing that side
and the road on that other side
was still opposite this.
Then – it happened
There is no question of this.
In fact – no one has questioned it at all.
Further proof of this comes from the police
who say that a woman held for questioning
was released immediately
because she didn't know any of the answers
to the questions that no one asked her . . .

So –
it's something of a mystery.
Yes –
it's a mysterious thing to some
and there are some who think
it could
in a mysterious way
be nothing at all.

Michael Rosen

The Forlorn Sea

Our Princess married
A fairy King,
It was a sensational
Wedding.

Now they live in a palace
Of porphyry,
Far, far away,
By the fòrlorn sea.

Sometimes people visit them,
Last week they invited me;
That is how I can tell you
They live by a fòrlorn sea.

(They said: Here's a magic carpet,
Come on this,
And when you arrive
We will give you a big kiss.)

I play in the palace garden,
I climb the sycamore tree,
Sometimes I swim
In the fòrlorn sea.

The King and the Princess are shadowy,
Yet beautiful,
They are waited on by white cats,
Who are dutiful.

It is like a dream
When they kiss and cuddle me,
But I like it, I like it,
I do not wish to break free.

So I eat all they give me
Because I have read
If you eat fairy food
You will never wake up in your own bed,

But will go on living,
As has happened to me,
Far, far away
By a fòrlorn sea.

Stevie Smith

Advice to a Knight

Wear modest armour; and walk quietly
In woods, where any noise is treacherous.
Avoid dragons and deceptive maidens.

Be polite to other men in armour,
Especially the fierce ones, who are often strong.
Treat all old men as they might be magicians.

So you may come back from you wanderings,
Clink proud and stiff into the queen's court
To doff your helmet and expect her thanks.

The young queen is amused at your white hair,
Asks you to show your notched and rusty sword,
And orders extra straw for your bedding.

Tomorrow put on your oldest clothes,
Take a stout stick and set off again,
It's safer that way if no more rewarding.

T. H. Jones

Old English Riddle

I'm by nature solitary, scarred by spear
and wounded by sword, weary of battle.
I frequently see the face of war, and fight
hateful enemies; yet I hold no hope
of help being brought to me in the battle,
before I'm eventually done to death.
In the stronghold of the city sharp-edged swords,
skilfully forged in the flame by smiths,
bite deeply into me. I can but await
a more fearsome encounter; it is not for me
to discover in the city any of those doctors
who heal grievous wounds with roots and herbs.
The scars from sword wounds gape wider and wider;
death blows are dealt me by day and by night.

Translated by Kevin Crossley-Holland

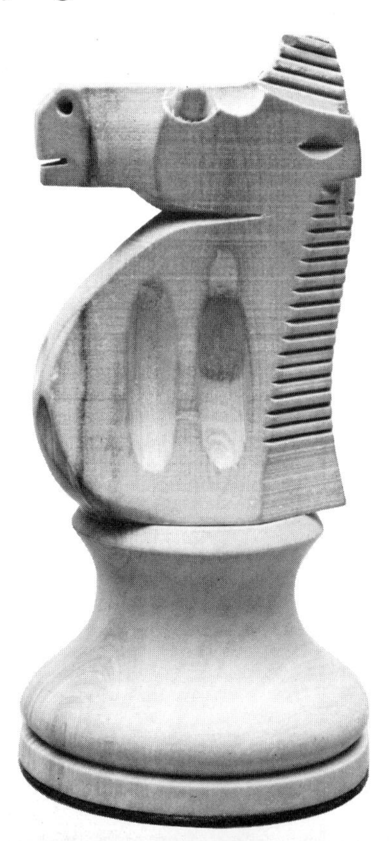

Goody Blake and Harry Gill
A True Story

Oh! what's the matter? what's the matter?
What is't that ails young Harry Gill?
That evermore his teeth they chatter,
Chatter, chatter, chatter still!
At night, at morning, and at noon,
'Tis all the same with Harry Gill;
Beneath the sun, beneath the moon,
His teeth they chatter, chatter still!

Young Harry was a lusty drover,
And who so stout of limb as he?
His cheeks were red as ruddy clover;
His voice was like the voice of three.
Old Goody Blake was old and poor;
Ill fed she was, and thinly clad;
And any man who passed her door
Might see how poor a hut she had.

Remote from sheltered village-green,
On a hill's northern side she dwelt,
Where from sea-blasts the hawthorns lean,
And hoary dews are slow to melt.
'Twas well enough, when summer came,
The long, warm, lightsome summer-day,
Then at her door the canty Dame
Would sit, as any linnet, gay.

But when the ice our streams did fetter,
Oh then how her old bones would shake!
You would have said, if you had met her,
'Twas a hard time for Goody Blake.
Her evenings then were dull and dead:
Sad case it was, as you may think,
For very cold to go to bed;
And then for cold not sleep a wink.

Now, when the frost was past enduring,
And made her poor old bones to ache,
Could anything be more alluring
Than the old hedge to Goody Blake?
And now and then, it must be said,
When her old bones were cold and chill,
She left her fire or left her bed,
To seek the hedge of Harry Gill.

Now Harry he had long suspected
This trespass of old Goody Blake;
And vowed that she should be detected –
That he on her would vengeance take.
And oft from his warm fire he'd go,
And to the fields his road would take,
And there, at night, in frost and snow,
He watch'd to seize old Goody Blake.

And once, behind a rick of barley,
Thus looking out did Harry stand:
The moon was full and shining clearly,
And crisp with frost the stubble land.
– He hears a noise – he's all awake –
Again? – on tip-toe down the hill
He softly creeps – 'tis Goody Blake;
She's at the hedge of Harry Gill!

Right glad was he when he beheld her:
Stick after stick did Goody pull,
He stood behind a bush of elder,
Till she had filled her apron full.
When with her load she turned about,
The by-way back again to take;
He started forward, with a shout,
And sprang upon poor Goody Blake.

And fiercely by the arm he took her,
And by the arm he held her fast,
And fiercely by the arm he shook her,
And cried, 'I've caught you then at last!'
Then Goody, who had nothing said,
Her bundle from her lap let fall;
And kneeling on the sticks, she prayed
To God that is the judge of all.

She prayed, her withered hand uprearing,
While Harry held her by the arm –
'God! who are never out of hearing,
O may he never more be warm!'
The cold, cold moon above her head,
Thus on her knees did Goody pray;
Young Harry heard what she had said:
And icy cold he turned away.

He went complaining all the morrow
That he was cold and very chill:
His face was gloom, his heart was sorrow,
Alas! that day for Harry Gill!
And Harry's flesh it fell away;
And all who see him say, 'tis plain,
That, live as long as live he may,
He never will be warm again.

No word to any man he utters,
A-bed or up, to young or old;
But ever to himself he mutters,
'Poor Harry Gill is very cold.'
A-bed or up, by night or day;
His teeth they chatter, chatter still.
Now think, ye farmers all, I pray,
Of Goody Blake and Harry Gill!

William Wordsworth

Saturdays I put on my boots and go wading
down the River Pinn
singing songs like: Olly Jonathan Curly and Carrot
past garden trees, the back of shops, building sites
scaffolds and timber, park-keepers' huts
the disused railway line and the new estate
the garage junk heap, twenty foot high in greasy
springs
unstuffed car-seats, boxes in thousands
light bulbs, rubber stamps and an old typewriter,
through the woods where the woodpeckers used to be
and there are rapids and bogs and sand-flats,
you have to watch for hidden jaws in the mud
or beaver dams and Amazon settlements;
you can see into the back of the telephone exchange
to a million wires on the walls
and an all-red telephone
and there's Grolly's Grotto:
the tunnel under the library under the cleaners
under the bicycle sheds and the newspaper stand.
In the middle it smells black,
you can't see either end
the walls are wet and the water's deeper
where Thatcher fell in and under
and screamed for hours so it echoed and echoed
but we couldn't see him –

all we could hear was him splashing and thrashing
hitting the walls with his boots
us holding on to the mucky bricks
bumping into each other's arms
or shouting and shushing until it went quiet
and still in the dark. And then we ran.
Or swam. And fought. It was miles.
Rushed into the light covered in slime
looking at each other with eyes big and silly:
Where's Thatcher?
No one said we'd left him. Just us goggling –
waiting for a splosh or scud.
It was raining where we stood
goggling in the light under the library where it was
warm
not knowing that Thatcher was crawling out the other
end

Michael Rosen

The Galloping Cat

Oh I am a cat that likes to
Gallop about doing good
So
One day when I was
Galloping about doing good, I saw
A Figure in the path; I said:
Get off! (Be-
  cause
I am a cat that likes to
Gallop about doing good)
But he did not move, instead
He raised his hand as if
To land me a cuff
So I made to dodge so as to
Prevent him bringing it orf,
Un-for-tune-ately I slid
On a banana skin
Some Ass had left instead
Of putting in the bin. So
His hand caught me on the cheek
I tried
To lay his arm open from wrist to elbow
With my sharp teeth
Because I am
A cat that likes to gallop about doing good.
Would you believe it?
He wasn't there
My teeth met nothing but air,
But a Voice said: Poor cat,
(Meaning me) and a soft stroke
Came on me head
Since when I have been bald.
I regard myself as
A martyr to doing good.

Also I heard a swoosh
As of wings, and saw
A halo shining at the height of
Mrs Gubbin's backyard fence,
So I thought: What's the good
Of galloping about doing good
When angels stand in the path
And do not do as they should
Such as having an arm to be bitten off.
All the same I
Intend to go on being
A cat that likes to
Gallop about doing good
So
With my bald head I go,
Chopping the untidy flowers down, to and fro,
An' scooping up the grass to show
Underneath
The cinderpath of wrath
Ha ha ha ha, ho,
Angels aren't the only who do not know
What's what and that
Galloping about doing good
Is a full-time job
That needs
An experienced eye of earthly
Sharpness, worth I dare say
(If you'll forgive a personal note)
A good deal more
Than all that skyey stuff
Of angels that make so bold as
To pity a cat like me that
Gallops about doing good.

Stevie Smith

Glasgow October 1972

At the Old Ship Bank pub in Saltmarket
a milk-lapping contest is in progress.
A dozen very assorted Bridgeton cats
have sprung from their starting-blocks
to get their heads down in the gleaming saucers.
In the middle of the picture
young Tiny is about to win his bottle of whisky
by kittening through the sweet half-gill
in one minute forty seconds flat, but
Sarah, at the end of the line,
self-contained and silver-grey,
has sat down with her back to the saucer
and surveys the photographers calmly.
She is a cat who does not like milk.

Edwin Morgan

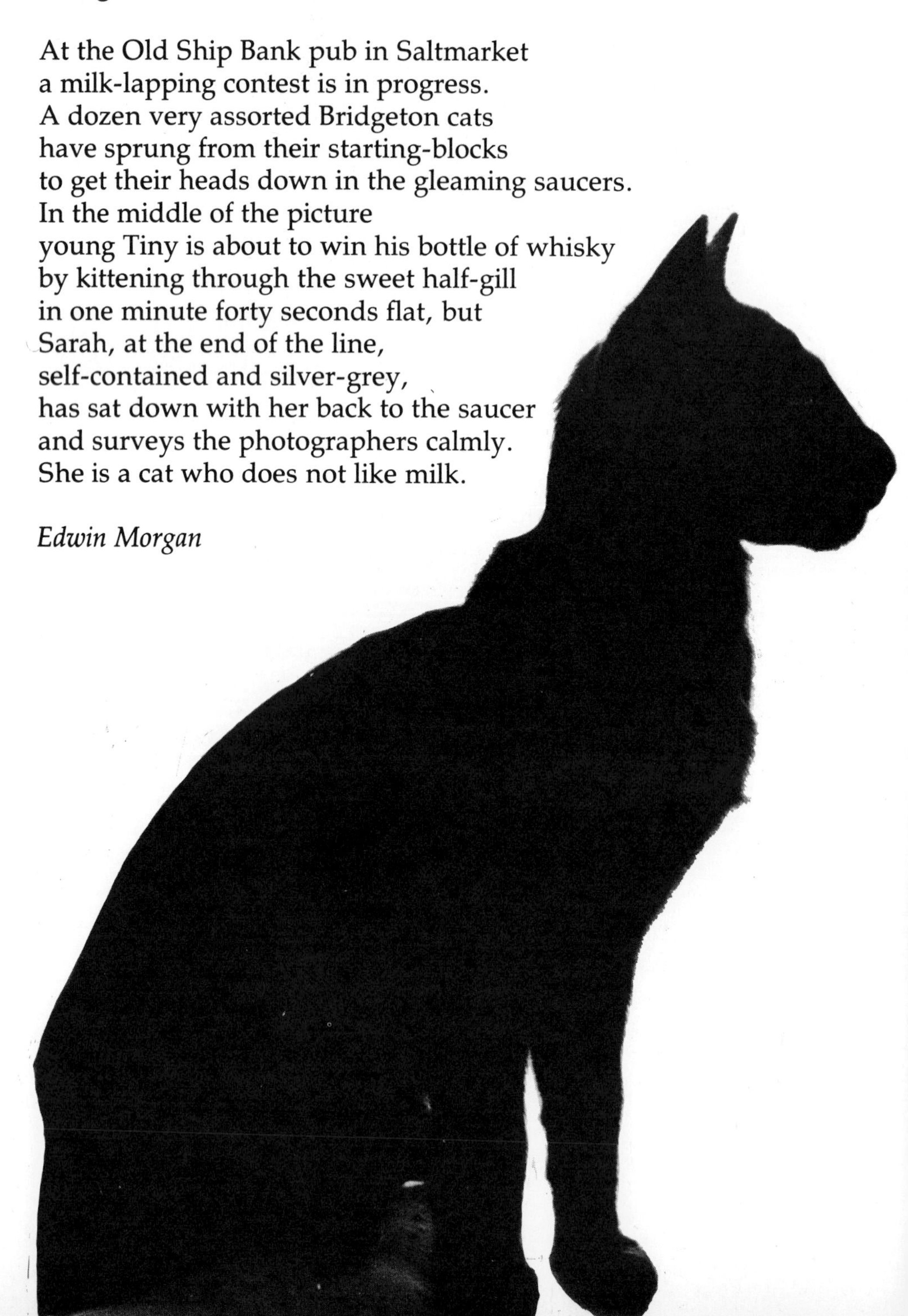

Milk for the Cat

When the tea is brought at five o'clock,
And all the neat curtains are drawn with care,
The little black cat with bright green eyes
Is suddenly purring there.

At first she pretends, having nothing to do,
She has come in merely to blink by the grate,
But, though tea may be late or the milk may be sour
She is never late.

And presently her agate eyes
Take a soft, large, milky haze
And her independent casual glance
Becomes a stiff, hard gaze.

Then she stamps her claws or lifts her ears,
Or twists her tail and begins to stir,
Till suddenly all her lithe body becomes
One breathing, trembling purr.

The children eat and wriggle and laugh,
The two old ladies stroke their silk:
But the cat is grown small and thin with desire,
Transformed to a creeping lust for milk.

The white saucer like some full moon descends
At last from the clouds of the table above;
She sighs and dreams and thrills and glows,
Transfigured with love.

She nestles over the shining rim,
Buries her chin in the creamy sea;
Her tail hangs loose; each drowsy paw
Is doubled under each bending knee.

[cont

A long, dim ectasy holds her life;
Her world is an infinite shapeless white,
Till her tongue has curled the last holy drop,
Then she sinks back into the night,

Draws and dips her body to heap
Her sleepy nerves in the great arm-chair,
Lies defeated and buried deep
Three or four hours unconscious there.

Harold Monro

A Widow Bird

A widow bird sate mourning for her love
 Upon a wintry bough;
The frozen wind crept on above,
 The freezing stream below.

There was no leaf upon the forest bare,
 No flower upon the ground,
And little motion in the air
 Except the mill-wheel's sound.

Percy Bysshe Shelley

Fetching Cows

The black one, last as usual, swings her head
And coils a black tongue round a grass-tuft. I
Watch her soft weight come down, her split feet
        spread.

In front, the others swing and slouch; they roll
Their great Greek eyes and breathe out milky gusts
From muzzles black and shiny as wet coal.

The collie trots, bored, at my heels, then plops
Into the ditch. The sea makes a tired sound
That's always stopping though it never stops.

A haycart squats prickeared against the sky.
Hay breath and milk breath. Far out in the West
The wrecked sun founders though its colours fly.

The collie's bored. There's nothing to control . . .
And the black cow is two native carriers
Bringing its belly home, slung from a pole.

Norman MacCaig

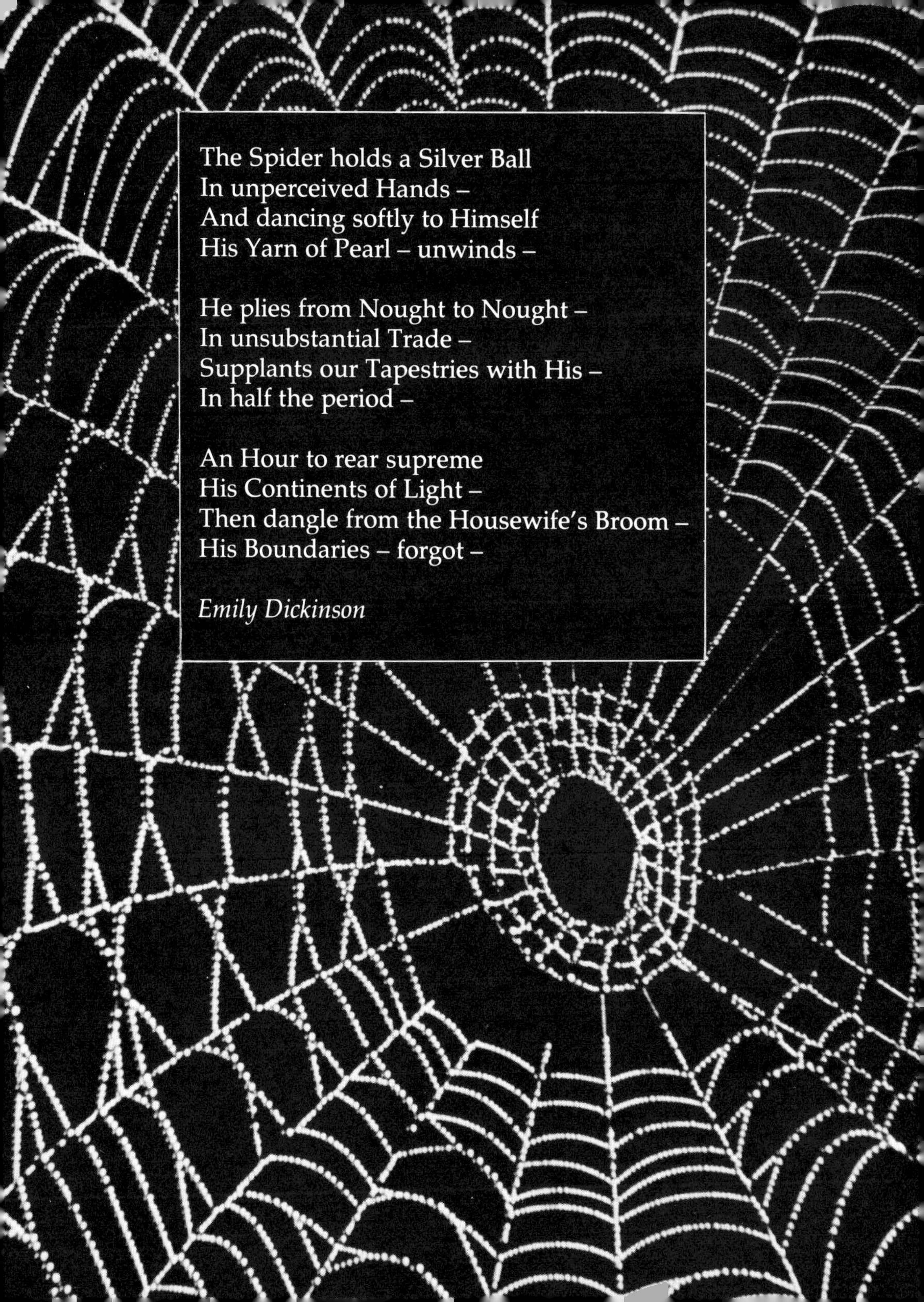

The Spider holds a Silver Ball
In unperceived Hands –
And dancing softly to Himself
His Yarn of Pearl – unwinds –

He plies from Nought to Nought –
In unsubstantial Trade –
Supplants our Tapestries with His –
In half the period –

An Hour to rear supreme
His Continents of Light –
Then dangle from the Housewife's Broom –
His Boundaries – forgot –

Emily Dickinson

The Wind begun to rock the Grass
With threatening Tunes and low –
He threw a Menace at the Earth –
A Menace at the Sky.

The Leaves unhooked themselves from Trees –
And started all abroad
The Dust did scoop itself like Hands
And threw away the Road.

The Wagons quickened on the Streets
The Thunder hurried slow –
The Lightning showed a Yellow Beak
And then a livid Claw.

The Birds put up the Bars to Nests –
The Cattle fled to Barns –
There came one drop of Giant Rain
And then as if the Hands

That held the Dams had parted hold
The Waters Wrecked the Sky,
But overlooked my Father's House –
Just quartering a Tree –

Emily Dickinson

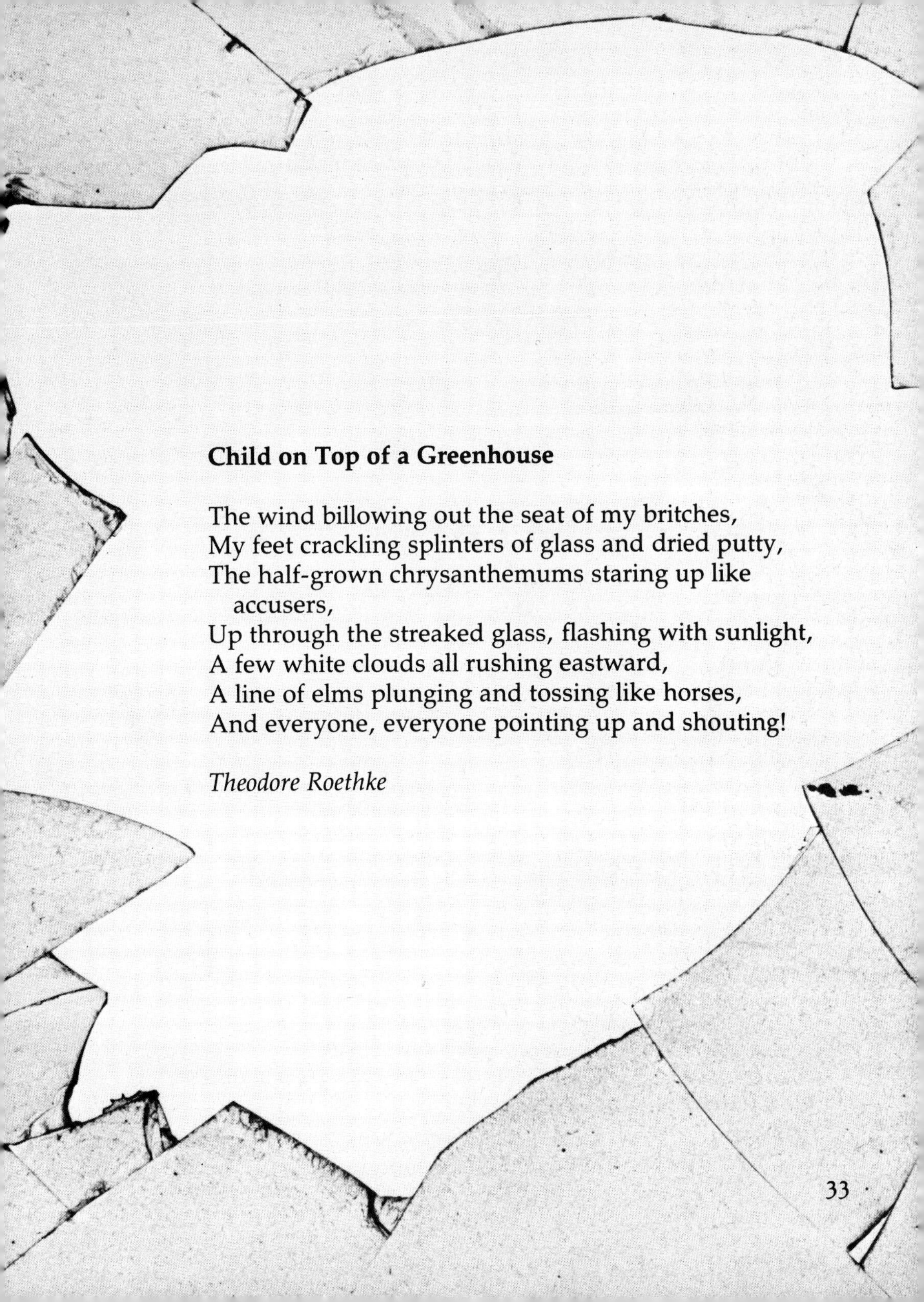

Child on Top of a Greenhouse

The wind billowing out the seat of my britches,
My feet crackling splinters of glass and dried putty,
The half-grown chrysanthemums staring up like
  accusers,
Up through the streaked glass, flashing with sunlight,
A few white clouds all rushing eastward,
A line of elms plunging and tossing like horses,
And everyone, everyone pointing up and shouting!

Theodore Roethke

Daysies

Now have I thereto this condicioun
That, of alle the flowers in the mede,
Than love I most these flowres whyte and rede,
Swiche as men callen daysies in our toun.
To hem have I so greet affeccioun,
As I seyde erst, when comen is the May,
That in my bed ther daweth me no day
That I nam up, and walking in the mede
To seen these floures agein the sonne sprede,
Whan it up-riseth by the morwe shene,
The longe day, thus walking in the grene,
And whan the sonne ginneth for to weste,
Than closeth hit, and draweth hit to reste.

. . . lening on myn elbowe and my syde
The long day I shoop me for to abyde
Fir nothing elles, and I shal nat lye,
But for to loke upon the dayeseye,
That wel by reson men hit calle may
The 'dayeseye' or elles the 'ye of day,'
The emperice and flour of flours alle.
I pray to God that faire mot she falle,
And alle that Loven floures, for her sake!

Geoffrey Chaucer

The Lily

The modest Rose puts forth a thorn,
The humble Sheep a threatening horn;
While the Lily white shall in Love delight,
Nor a thorn, nor a threat, stain her beauty bright.

William Blake

The Dandelion's pallid tube
Astonishes the Grass,
And Winter instantly becomes
An infinite Alas –

The tube uplifts a signal Bud
And then a shouting Flower,–
The Proclamation of the Suns
That sepulture is o'er.

Emily Dickinson

Mist in the Meadows

The evening o'er the meadow seems to stoop
More distant lessens the diminished spire
Mist in the hollows reaks and curdles up
Like fallen clouds that spread – and things retire
Less seen and less – the shepherd passes near
And little distant most grotesquely shades
As walking without legs – lost to his knees
As through the rawky creeping smoke he wades
Now half way up the arches disappear
And small the bits of sky that glimmer through
Then trees loose all but tops – while fields remain
As wont – the indistinctness passes bye
The shepherd all his length is seen again
And further on the village meets the eye.

John Clare

The Fog

I saw the fog grow thick
Which soon made blind my ken;
It made tall men of boys,
And giants of tall men.

It clutched my throat, I coughed;
Nothing was in my head
Except two heavy eyes
Like balls of burning lead.

And when it grew so black
That I could know no place,
I lost all judgement then
Of distance and of space.

The street lamps, and the lights
Upon the halted cars,
Could either be on earth
Or be the heavenly stars.

A man passed by me close,
I asked my way, he said,
'Come, follow me, my friend' –
I followed where he led.

He walked the stones in front,
'Trust me,' he said, 'and come':
I followed like a child –
A blind man led me home.

W H Davies

The fog comes
on little cat feet.
It sits looking
over harbor and city
on silent haunches
and then moves on.

Carl Sandburg

November Night, Edinburgh

The night tinkles like ice in glasses.
Leaves are glued to the pavement with frost.
The brown air fumes at the shop windows,
Tries the doors, and sidles past.

I gulp down winter raw. The heady
Darkness swirls with tenements.
In a brown fuzz of cottonwool
Lamps fade up crags, die into pits.

Frost in my lungs is harsh as leaves
Scraped up on paths. I look up, there,
A high roof sails, at the mast-head
Fluttering a grey and ragged star.

The world's a bear shrugged in his den.
It's snug and close in the snoring night.
And outside like chrysanthemums
The fog unfolds its bitter scent.

Norman MacCaig

Friday Morning

It was on a Friday morning that they took me from the
  cell,
And I saw they had a carpenter to crucify as well:
You can blame it on to Pilate, you can blame it on the
  Jews,
You can blame it on the devil, but it's God I accuse.

'It's God they ought to crucify instead of you and me,'
I said it to the carpenter a-hanging on the tree.

You can blame it on to Adam, you can blame it on to
  Eve,
You can blame it on the apple, but that I can't believe;
It was God who made the devil and the woman and
  the man,
But there wouldn't be an apple if it wasn't in the plan.

Now Barabbas was a killer, and they let Barabbas go,
But you are being crucified for nothing here below,
And God is up in heaven, but he doesn't do a thing,
With a million angels watching, and they never move
  a wing.

'To hell with Jehovah!' to the carpenter I said,
'I wish that a carpenter had made the world instead.
Good-bye and good luck to you, our ways they will
  divide,
Remember me in heaven, the man you hung beside.'

Sydney Carter

The Carol of the Poor Children

We are the poor children, come out to see the sights
On this day of all days, on this night of nights,
The stars in merry parties are dancing in the sky,
A fine star, a new star, is shining on high!

We are the poor children, our lips are frosty blue,
We cannot sing our carol as well as rich folk do,
Our bellies are so empty we have no singing voice,
But this night of all nights good children must rejoice.

We do rejoice, we do rejoice, as hard as we can try,
A fine star, a new star is shining in the sky!
And while we sing our carol, we think of the delight
The happy kings and shepherds make in Bethlehem
tonight.

Are we naked, mother, and are we starving-poor –
Oh, see what gifts the kings have brought outside the
stable door,
Are we cold, mother, the ass will give his hay
To make the manger warm and keep the cruel winds
away.

We are the poor children, but not so poor who sing
Our carol with our voiceless hearts to greet the
new-born king,
On this night of all nights, when in the frosty sky
A new star, a kind star is shining on high!

Richard Middleton

Epitaph in Lydford Churchyard

Here lies in a horizontal position the outside case of

GEORGE ROUTLEDGE, WATCHMAKER

Integrity was the mainspring and prudence
the regulator of all the actions of his life;
humane, generous and liberal,
His hand never stopped till he had relieved distress.

So nicely regulated were his movements that
he never went wrong, except when set going by
people who did not know his key.
Even then he was easily set right again.
He had the art of disposing his time so well,
till his hours glided away, his pulse
stopped beating.

He ran down November 14, 1801, aged 57,
In hopes of being taken in hand by his Maker,
Thoroughly cleaned, repaired, wound up, and set
going in the world to come, when time shall be no
more.

Song

When I am dead, my dearest,
  Sing no sad songs for me;
Plant thou no roses at my head,
  Nor shady cypress tree:
Be the green grass above me
  With showers and dewdrops wet;
And if thou wilt, remember,
  And if thou wilt, forget.
I shall not see the shadows,
  I shall not feel the rain;
I shall not hear the nightingale
  Sing on, as if in pain:
And dreaming through the twilight
  That doth not rise nor set,
Haply I may remember,
  And haply may forget.

Christina Rossetti

IN MEMORY OF
WILLIAM PICKERING,
who died Decʀ 24. 1845
AGED 30 YEARS.
ALSO RICHARD EDGER
who died Decʀ 24. 1845
AGED 24 YEARS.
THE SPIRITUAL RAILWAY
The Line to heaven by Christ was made
With heavenly truth the Rails are laid,
From Earth to Heaven the Line extends,
To Life Eternal where it ends.
Repentance is the Station then
Where Passengers are taken in
No Fee for them is there to pay
For Jesus is himself the way.
God's Word is the first Engineer
It points the way to Heaven so dear,
Through tunnels dark and dreary here
It does the way to Glory steer.
God's Love the Fire, his Truth the Steam,
Which drives the Engine and the Train,
All you who would to Glory ride,
Must come to Christ, in him abide
In First, and Second, and Third Class,
Repentance, Faith and Holiness,
You must the way to Glory gain
Or you with Christ will not remain.
Come then poor Sinners, now's the time
At any Station on the Line,
If you'll repent and turn from sin
The Train will stop and take you in.

Requiem

Under the wide and starry sky,
Dig the grave and let me lie.
Glad did I live and gladly die,
   And I laid me down with a will.

This be the verse you grave for me:
Here he lies where he longed to be;
Home is the sailor, home from sea,
   And the hunter home from the hill.

Robert Louis Stevenson

Here lies a poor woman who always was tired,
   She lived in a house where no help wasn't hired.
The last words she said were 'Dear friends, I am going,
   Where washing ain't wanted, nor mending, nor
   sewing.
There all things is done just exact to my wishes,
   For where folk don't eat there's no washing of
   dishes.
In Heaven loud anthems for ever are ringing,
   But having no voice, I'll keep clear of the singing.
Don't mourn for me now, don't mourn for me never;
   I'm going to do nothing for ever and ever.'

An Inscription by the Sea

(after the Greek of Glaucos)

No dust have I to cover me,
   My grave may no man show;
My tomb is this unending sea,
   And I lie far below.
My fate, O stranger, was to drown;
And where it was the ship went down
   Is what the sea-birds know.

The Express

After the first powerful plain manifesto
The black statement of pistons, without more fuss
But gliding like a queen, she leaves the station.
Without bowing and with restrained unconcern
She passes the houses which humbly crowd outside,
The gasworks, and at last the heavy page
Of death, printed by gravestones in the cemetery.
Beyond the town there lies the open country
Where, gathering speed, she acquires mystery,
The luminous self-possession of ships on ocean.
It is now she begins to sing – at first quite low
Then loud, and at last with a jazzy madness –
The song of her whistle screaming at curves,
Of deafening tunnels, brakes, innumerable bolts.
And always light, aerial, underneath,
Retreats the elate metre of her wheels.
Steaming through metal landscape on her lines,
She plunges new eras of white happiness,
Where speed throws up strange shapes, broad curves
And parallels clean like the steel of guns.
At last, further than Edinburgh or Rome,
Beyond the crest of the world, she reaches night
Where only a low streamline brightness
Of phosphorus on the tossing hills is white.
Ah, like a comet through flame she moves entranced
Wrapt in her music no bird song, no, nor bough
Breaking with honey buds, shall ever equal.

Stephen Spender

A Local Train of Thought

Alone, in silence, at a certain time of night,
Listening, and looking up from what I'm trying to
  write,
I hear a local train along the Valley. And 'There
Goes the one-fifty', think I to myself; aware
That somehow its habitual travelling comforts me,
Making my world seem safer, homelier, sure to be
The same to-morrow; and the same, one hopes, next
  year.
'There's peacetime in that train.' One hears it
  disappear
With needless warning whistle and rail-resounding
  wheels.
'That train's quite like an old familiar friend', one feels.

Siegfried Sassoon

Tremors

We took turns at laying
An ear on the rail –
So that we could tell
By the vibrations

When a train was coming.
Then we'd flatten ourselves
To the banks, scorched
Vetch and hedge-parsley,

While the iron flanks
Rushed past, sending sparks
Flying. It is more and more
A question of living

With an ear to the ground:
The tremors, when they come,
Are that much greater –
For ourselves, and others.

Nor is it any longer
A game, but a matter
Of survival: each explosion
Part of a procession

There can be no stopping.
Though the end is known,
There is nothing for it
But to keep listening . . .

Stewart Conn

Midnight on the Great Western

In the third-class seat sat the journeying boy,
  And the roof-lamp's oily flame
Played down on his listless form and face,
Bewrapt past knowing to what he was going,
  Or whence he came.

In the band of his hat the journeying boy
  Had a ticket stuck; and a string
Around his neck bore the key of his box,
That twinkled gleams of the lamp's sad beams
  Like a living thing.

What past can be yours, O journeying boy
  Towards a world unknown,
Who calmly, as if incurious quite
On all at stake, can undertake
  This plunge alone?

Knows your soul a sphere, O journeying boy
  Our rude realms far above,
Whence with spacious vision you mark and mete
This region of sin that you find you in
  But are not of?

Thomas Hardy

Corner Seat

Suspended in a moving night
The face in the reflected train
Looks at first sight as self-assured
As your own face. But look again.
Windows between you and the world
Keep out the cold, keep out the fright.
Then why does your reflection seem
So lonely in the moving night?

Louis MacNeice

To a Fat Lady Seen from the Train

O why do you walk through the fields in gloves,
  Missing so much and so much?
O fat white woman whom nobody loves,
Why do you walk through the fields in gloves,
When the grass is soft as the breast of doves
  And shivering-sweet to the touch?
O why do you walk through the fields in gloves,
  Missing so much and so much.

Frances Cornford

The Fear of Flowers

The nodding oxeye bends before the wind,
The woodbine quakes lest boys their flowers should
find,
And prickly dogrose spite of its array
Can't dare the blossom-seeking hand away,
While thistles wear their heavy knobs of bloom
Proud as a warhorse wears its haughty plume,
And by the roadside danger's self defy;
On commons where pined sheep and oxen lie
In ruddy pomp and ever thronging mood
It stands and spreads like danger in a wood,
And in the village street where meanest weeds
Can't stand untouched to fill their husks with seeds,
The haughty thistle o'er all danger towers,
In every place the very wasp of flowers.

John Clare

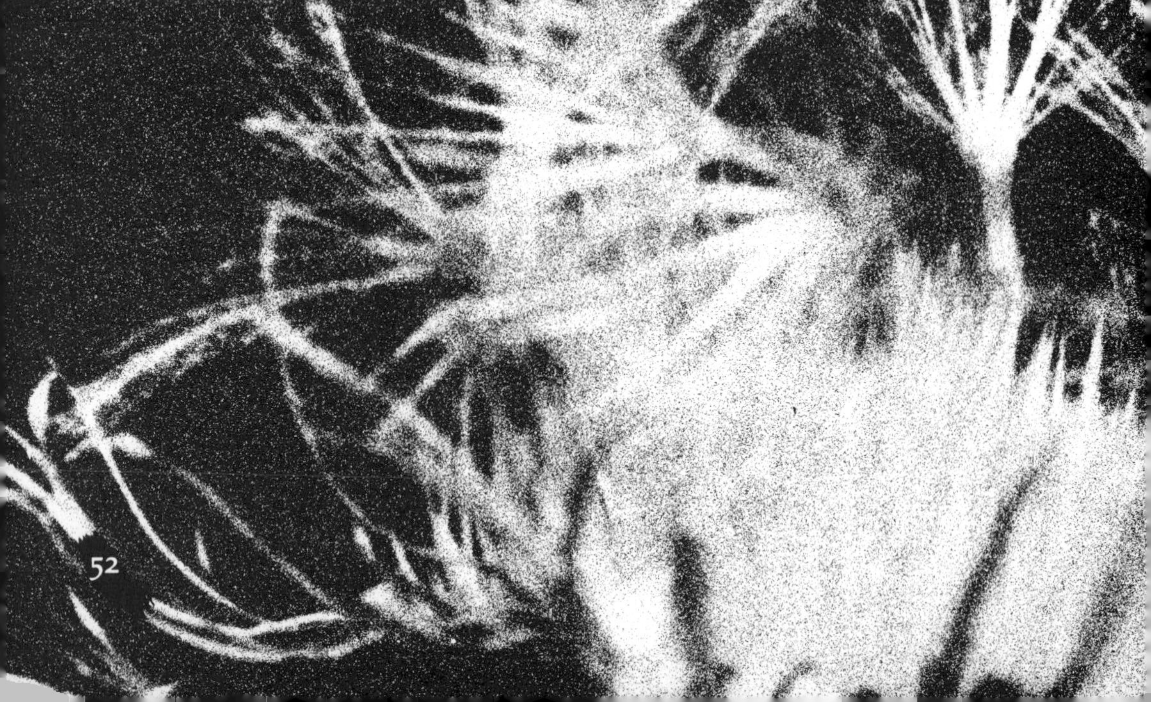

Thistledown

Silver against blue sky
These ghosts of day float by,
Fitful, irregular,
Each one a silk-haired star,
Till from the wind's aid freed
They settle on their seed.

Not by the famished light
Of a moon-ridden night
But by clear sunny hours
Gaily these ghosts of flowers
Will rise and swirl and fall
Dance to their burial.

Andrew Young

Thistle

Thistle, blue bunch of daggers
rattling upon the wind,
saw-tooth that separates
the lips of grasses.

Your wound in childhood was
a savage shock of joy
that set the bees on fire
and the loud larks singing.

Your head enchanted then
smouldering among the flowers
filled the whole sky with smoke
and sparks of seed.

Now from your stabbing bloom's
nostalgic point of pain
ghosts of those summers rise
rustling across my eyes.

Seeding a magic thorn
to prick the memory,
to start in my icy flesh
fevers of long lost fields.

Laurie Lee

Thistles

Against the rubber tongues of cows and the hoeing
hands of men
Thistles spike the summer air
Or crackle open under a blue-black pressure.

Every one a revengeful burst
Of resurrection, a grasped fistful
Of splintered weapons and Icelandic frost thrust up

From the underground stain of a decayed Viking.
They are like pale hair and the gutturals of dialects.
Every one manages a plume of blood.

Then they grow grey, like men.
Mown down, it is a feud. Their sons appear,
Stiff with weapons, fighting back over the same
ground.

Ted Hughes

Thistles

Half grown before half seen,
like urchins in armour
double their size they stand
their ground boldly, their keen
swords out. But the farmer
ignores them. Not a hand

will he lift to cut them down:
they are not worth his switch
he says. Uncertain whom
they challenge, having grown
into their armour, each
breaks out a purple plume.

Under this image
of their warrior blood
they make a good death,
meeting the farmer's blade
squarely in their old age.
White then as winter breath

from every white head
a soul springs up. The wind
is charged with spirits: no –
not spirits of the dead
for these are living, will land
at our backs and go

to ground. Farmer and scythe
sing to each other. He
cannot see how roots writhe
underfoot, how the sons
of this fallen infantry
will separate our bones.

Jon Stallworthy

Think of this tower-block
as if it was a street standing up
and instead of toing and froing
in buses and cars
you up and down it
in a high speed lift.

There will be no pavement artists of course
because there aren't any pavements.
There isn't room for a market
but then there isn't room for cars.
No cars: no accidents
but don't lean
out of the windows
don't play in the lifts
or they won't work.
They don't work
and they won't work
if you play Split Kipper,
Fox and Chickens, Dittyback,
Keek-bogle, Jackerback,
Huckey-buck, Hotchie-pig,
Foggy-plonks, Ching Chang Cholly
or Bunky-Bean Bam-Bye.

Go down. The stairs are outside –
you can't miss them – try not to miss them, please.
No pets.
Think how unhappy they'd be
locked in a tower-block.
There will be
no buskers, no hawkers
no flowers, no chinwaggers
no sandwich boards,
no passers-by,
except for
low-flying aircraft
or high-flying sparrows.

Here is a note from Head Office:
you will love your neighbour
left right above below
so no music, creaky boots,
caterwauling somersaulting –
never never never jump up or down
or you may
never never never get down or up again.
No questions.
It's best to tip-toe,
creep, crawl, and whisper.
If there *are* any
problems phone me
and I'll be out.
Good day.

Michael Rosen

NO PARKING
NO
PARKING

14

Number 14

That house you took me to
as a child, with its steps down
from the pavement into a doorway
that smelled of damp, along a passage
into a parlour with a black-leaded grate
and a brace of partridge in white
porcelain, that house
where you grew up under your father's belt –
I pass it every day, and up till now
I have watched the street it stood in
fall to the bulldozers, house by house
each day a bit more sky:
old man, the bulldozers have gone away
but your house is still there
its red front door still saying Number 14
its windows hooded with corrugated iron
jagged against the sky; its time come
and gone, waiting for one more stroke.

Keith Bosley

The Hammers

Noise of hammers once I heard,
Many hammers, busy hammers,
Beating, shaping, night and day,
Shaping, beating dust and clay
To a palace; saw it reared;
Saw the hammers laid away.

And I listened, and I heard
Hammers beating, night and day,
In the palace newly reared,
Beating it to dust and clay:
Other hammers, muffled hammers,
Silent hammers of decay.

Ralph Hodgson

Slough

Come, friendly bombs, and fall on Slough
It isn't fit for humans now,
There isn't grass to graze a cow
        Swarm over, Death!

Come, bombs, and blow to smithereens
Those air-conditioned, bright canteens,
Tinned fruit, tinned meat, tinned milk, tinned be
        Tinned minds, tinned breath.

Mess up the mess they call a town –
A house for ninety-seven down
And once a week a half a crown
        For twenty years,

And get that man with double chin
Who'll always cheat and always win,
Who washes his repulsive skin
        In women's tears.

And smash his desk of polished oak
And smash his hands so used to stroke
And stop his boring dirty joke
        And make him yell.

But spare the bald young clerks who add
The profits of the stinking cad;
It's not their fault that they are mad,
        They've tasted Hell.

It's not their fault they do not know
The birdsong from the radio,
It's not their fault they often go
        To Maidenhead.

And talk of sports and makes of cars
In various bogus Tudor bars
And daren't look up and see the stars
        But belch instead.

In labour-saving homes, with care
Their wives frizz out peroxide hair
And dry it in synthetic air
        And paint their nails.

Come, friendly bombs, and fall on Slough
To get it ready for the plough.
The cabbages are coming now:
        The earth exhales.

John Betjeman

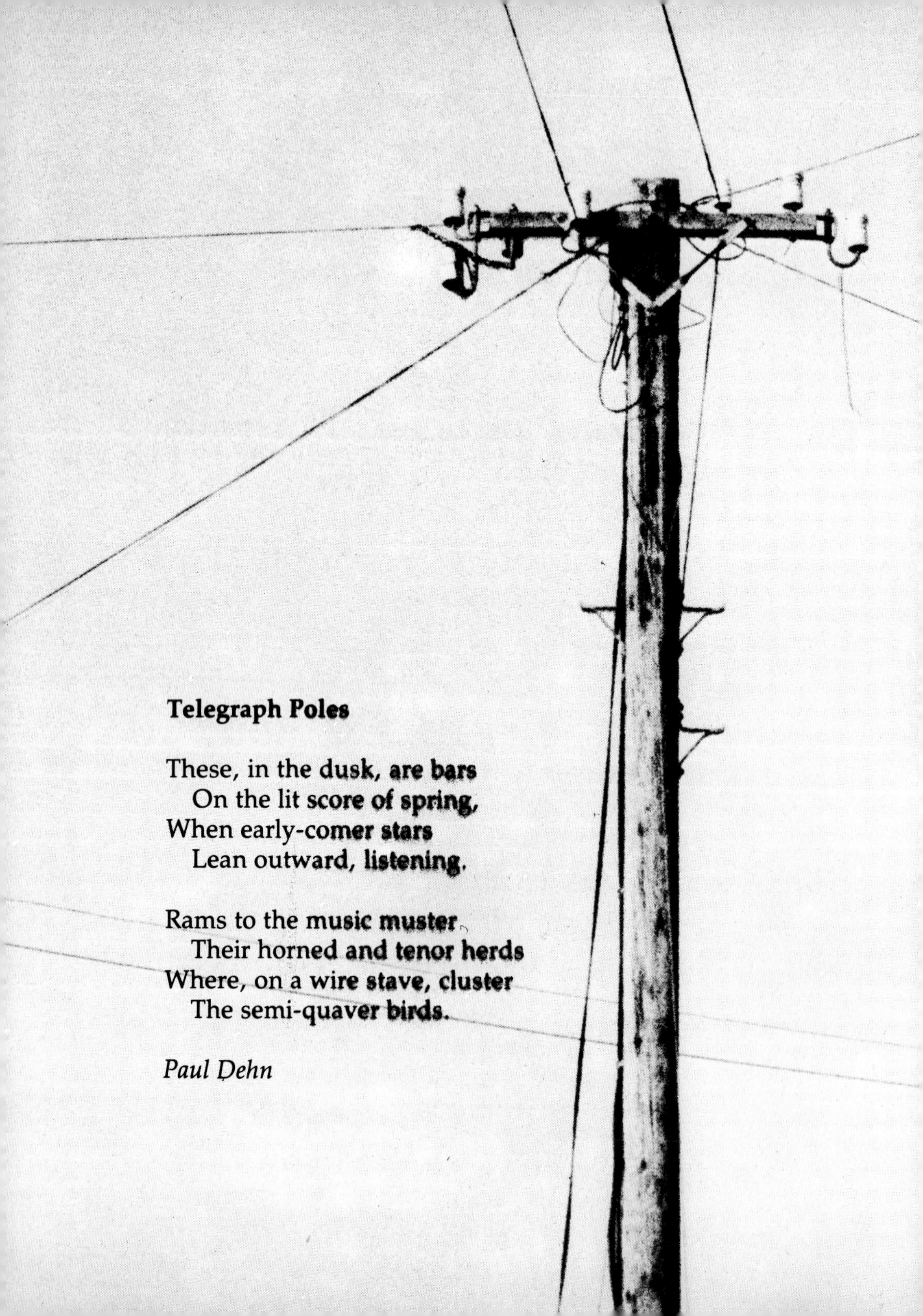

Telegraph Poles

These, in the dusk, are bars
On the lit score of spring,
When early-comer stars
Lean outward, listening.

Rams to the music muster
Their horned and tenor herds
Where, on a wire stave, cluster
The semi-quaver birds.

Paul Dehn

The Pylons

The secret of these hills was stone, and cottages
Of that stone made,
And crumbling roads
That turned on sudden hidden villages.

Now over these small hills they have built the concrete
That trails black wire:
Pylons, those pillars
Bare like nude, giant girls that have no secret.

The valley with its gilt and evening look
And the green chestnut
Of customary root,
Are mocked dry like the parched bed of a brook.

But far above and far as sight endures
Like whips of anger
With lightning's danger
There runs the quick perspective of the future.

This dwarfs our emerald country by its trek
So tall with prophecy:
Dreaming of cities
Where often clouds shall lean their swan-white neck.

Stephen Spender

Once at Piertarvit

Once at Piertarvit,
one day in April,
the edge of spring,
with the air a-ripple,
a sea like knitting,
as Avril and Ann
and Ian and I
walked in the wind
along the headland,
Ian threw an apple
high over Piertarvit.

Not a great throw,
you would say, if you saw it,
but good for Ian.
His body tautened,
his arm let go
like a flesh-and-bone bow,
and the hard brown apple
left over from autumn
flew up and up,
crossing our gaze
from the cliff at Piertarvit.

Then, all at once, horror
glanced off our eyes,
Ann's, mine, Avril's.
As the apple curved
in the stippled sky,
at the top of its arc,
it suddenly struck
the shape of a bird –
a gull that had glided
down from nowhere
above Piertarvit.

We imagined the thud
and the thin ribs breaking,
blood, and the bird
hurtling downward.
No such thing.
The broad wings wavered
a moment only,
then air sustained them.
The gull glided on
while the apple fell
in the sea at Piertarvit.

Nobody laughed.
Nobody whistled.
In that one moment,
our world had faltered.
The four of us stood
stock-still with horror,
till, breaking the spell,
Ian walked away
with a whirl in his head.
The whole sky curdled
over Piertarvit.

I followed slowly,
with Ann and Avril
trailing behind.
We had lost our lightness.
Even today,
old as we are,
we would find it hard
to say, without wonder,
'Ian hit a bird
with an apple, in April,
once at Piertarvit.'

Alastair Reid

Song

I had a dove and the sweet dove died;
And I have thought it died of grieving:
O, what could it grieve for? Its feet were tied,
With a silken thread of my own hand's weaving;
Sweet little red feet! why should you die –
Why should you leave me, sweet bird! why?
You lived alone in the forest-tree,
Why, pretty thing! would you not live with me?
I kissed you oft and gave you white peas;
Why not live sweetly, as in the green trees?

John Keats

Numbers

A thousand and fifty-one waves
Two hundred and thirty-one seagulls
A cliff of four hundred feet
Three miles of ploughed fields
One house
Four windows look on the waves
Four windows look on the ploughed fields
One skylight looks on the sky
In that skylight's sky is one seagull.

Stevie Smith

The Dog Lovers

So they bought you
And kept you in a
Very good home
Central heating
TV
A deep freeze
A *very* good home –
No one to take you
For that lovely long run –
But otherwise
'A *very* good home'.
They fed you Pal and Chum
But not that lovely long run,
Until, mad with energy and boredom
You escaped – and ran and ran and ran
Under a car.
Today they will cry for you –
Tomorrow they will buy another dog.

Spike Milligan

My Mother saw a Dancing Bear

My mother saw a dancing bear
By the schoolyard, a day in June.
The keeper stood with chain and bar
And whistle pipe, and played a tune.

And bruin lifted up its head
And lifted up its dusty feet,
And all the children laughed to see
It caper in the summer heat.

They watched as for the Queen it died.
They watched it march. They watched it halt.
They heard the keeper as he cried,
'Now, roly-poly!' 'Somersault!'

And then, my mother said, there came
The keeper with a begging-cup,
The bear with burning coat of fur,
Shaming the laughter to a stop.

They paid a penny for the dance,
But what they saw was not the show;
Only, in bruin's aching eyes,
Far-distant forests, and the snow.

Charles Causley

Song of the Battery Hen

We can't grumble about accommodation:
we have a new concrete floor that's
always dry, four walls that are
painted white, and a sheet-iron roof
the rain drums on. A fan blows warm air
beneath our feet to disperse the smell
of chicken-shit and, on dull days,
fluorescent lighting sees us.

You can tell me: if you come by
the North door, I am in the twelfth pen
on the left-hand side of the third row
from the floor; and in that pen
I am usually the middle one of three.
But, even without directions, you'd
discover me. I have the same orange-
red comb, yellow beak and auburn
feathers, but as the door opens and you
hear above the electric fan a kind of
one-word wail, I am the one
who sounds loudest in my head.

Listen. Outside this house there's an
orchard with small moss-green apple
trees; beyond that, two fields of
cabbages; then, on the far side of
the road, a broiler house. Listen:
one cockerel grows out of there, as
tall and proud as the first hour of sun.
Sometimes I stop calling with the others
to listen, and wonder if he hears me.

The next time you come here, look for me.
Notice the way I sound inside my head.
God made us all quite differently,
and blessed us with this expensive home.

Edwin Brock

One summer evening (led by her) I found
A little boat tied to a willow tree
Within a rocky cave, its usual home.
Straight I unloosed her chain, and stepping in
Pushed from the shore. It was an act of stealth
And troubled pleasure, nor without the voice
Of mountain-echoes did my boat move on;
Leaving behind her still, on either side,

Small circles glittering idly in the moon,
Until they melted all into one track
Of sparkling light. But now, like one who rows,
Proud of his skill, to reach a chosen point
With an unswerving line, I fixed my view
Upon the summit of a craggy ridge,
The horizon's utmost boundary; far above
Was nothing but the stars and the grey sky.
She was an elfin pinnace; lustily
I dipped my oars into the silent lake,
And, as I rose upon the stroke, my boat
Went heaving through the water like a swan;
When, from behind that craggy steep till then
The horizon's bound, a huge peak, black and huge,
As if with voluntary power instinct
Upreared its head. I struck and struck again,
And growing still in stature the grim shape
Towered up between me and the stars, and still,
For so it seemed, with purpose of its own
And measured motion like a living thing,
Strode after me. With trembling oars I turned,
And through the silent water stole my way
Back to the covert of the willow tree;
There in her mooring-place I left my bark, –
And through the meadows homeward went, in grave
And serious mood; but after I had seen
That spectacle, for many days, my brain
Worked with a dim and undetermined sense
Of unknown modes of being; o'er my thoughts
There hung a darkness, call it solitude
Or blank desertion. No familiar shapes
Remained, no pleasant images of trees,
Of sea or sky, no colours of green fields;
But huge and mighty forms, that do not live
Like living men, moved slowly through the mind
By day, and were a trouble to my dreams.

William Wordsworth from *The Prelude*

Stanzas

When a man hath no freedom to fight for at home,
   Let him combat for that of his neighbours;
Let him think of the glories of Greece and of Rome,
   And get knocked on the head for his labours.

To do good to mankind is the chivalrous plan,
   And is always as nobly requited;
Then battle for freedom wherever you can,
   And, if not shot or hanged, you'll get knighted.

Lord Byron

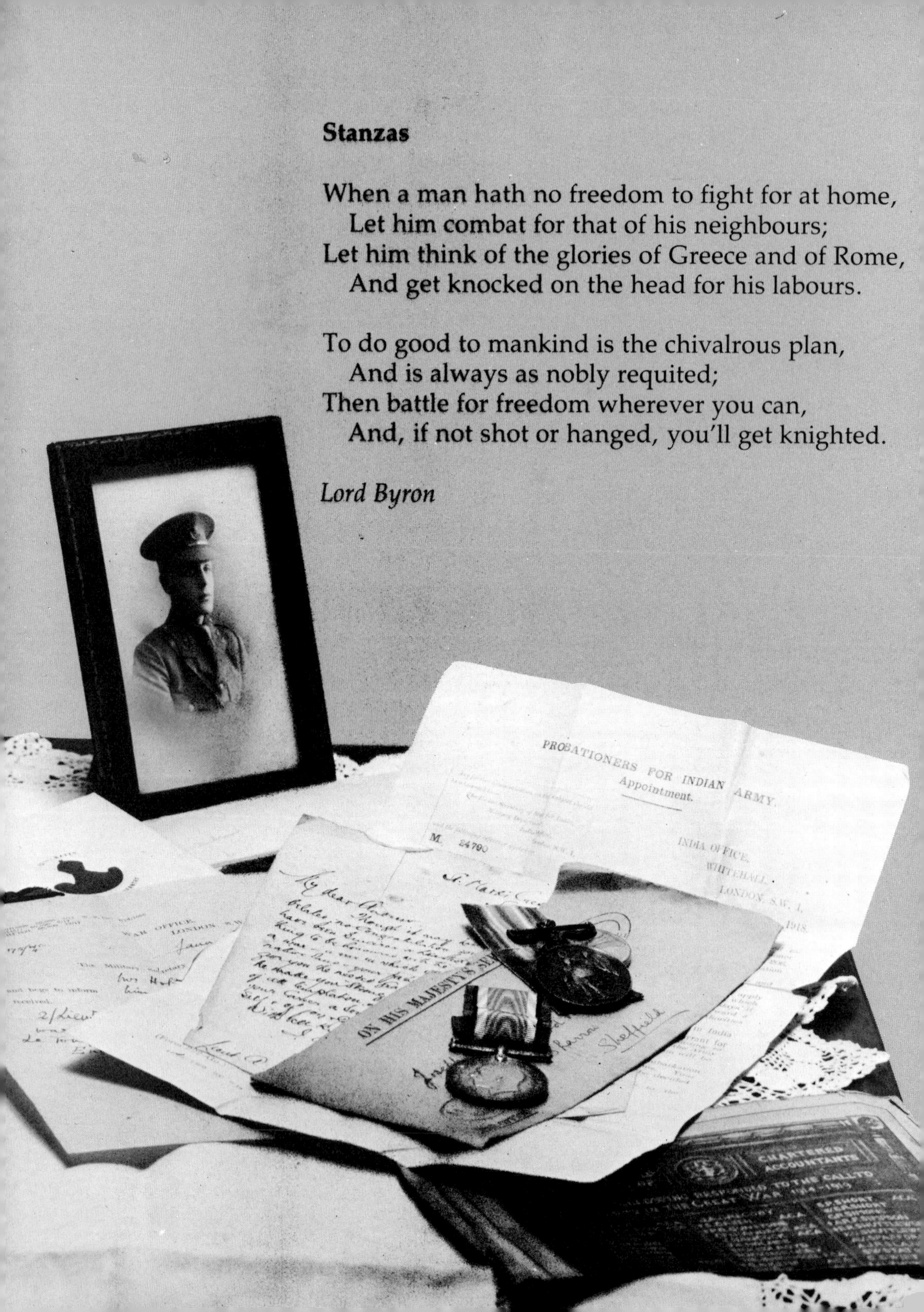

Harp Song of the Dane Women

What is a woman that you forsake her,
And the hearth-fire and the home-acre,
To go with the old grey Widow-maker?

She has no house to lay a guest in –
But one chill bed for all to rest in,
That the pale suns and the stray bergs nest in:

She has no strong white arms to fold you,
But the ten-times-fingering weed to hold you –
Out on the rocks where the tide has rolled you.

Yet, when the signs of summer thicken,
And the ice breaks, and the birch-buds quicken,
Yearly you turn from our side, and sicken –

Sicken again for the shouts and the slaughters.
You steal away to the lapping waters,
And look at your ship in her winter-quarters.

You forget our mirth, and talk at the tables,
The kine in the shed and the horse in the stables –
To pitch her sides and go over her cables.

Then you drive out where the storm-clouds swallow,
And the sound of your oar-blades, falling hollow,
Is all we have left through the months to follow.

Ah, what is Woman that you forsake her,
And the hearth-fire and the home-acre,
To go with the old grey Widow-maker?

Rudyard Kipling

Abbey Tomb

I told them not to ring the bells
The night the Vikings came
Out of the sea and passed us by.
The fog was thick as cream
And in the abbey we stood still
As if our breath might blare
Or pulses rattle if we once
Stopped staring at the door

Through the walls and through the fog
We heard them passing by.
The deafer monks thanked God too soon
And later only I
Could catch the sound of prowling men
Still present in the hills
So everybody else agreed
To ring the abbey bells.

And even while the final clang
Still snored upon the air,
And while the ringers joked their way
Down round the spiral stair,
Before the spit of fervent prayer
Had dried into the stone
The raiders came back through the fog
And killed us one by one.

Father Abbot at the altar
Lay back with his knees
Doubled under him, caught napping
In the act of praise.
Brother John lay unresponsive
In the warming room.
The spiders came out for the heat
And then the rats for him.

Under the level of the sheep
Who graze here all the time
We lie now, under tourists' feet
Who in good weather come.
I told them not to ring the bells
But centuries of rain
And blustering have made their tombs
Look just as right as mine.

Patricia Beer

The War Song of Dinas Vawr

The mountain sheep are sweeter,
But the valley sheep are fatter;
We therefore deemed it meeter
To carry off the latter.
We made an expedition;
We met a host, and quelled it;
We forced a strong position,
And killed the men who held it.

On Dyfed's richest valley,
Where herds of kine were brousing,
We made a mighty sally,
To furnish our carousing.
Fierce warriors rushed to meet us;
We met them, and o'erthrew them:
They struggled hard to beat us;
But we conquered them, and slew them.

As we drove our prize at leisure,
The king marched forth to catch us:
His rage surpassed all measure,
But his people could not match us.
He fled to his hall-pillars;
And, ere our force we led off,
Some sacked his house and cellars,
While others cut his head off.

We there, in strife bewildering,
Spilt blood enough to swim in:
We orphaned many children,
And widowed many women.
The eagles and the ravens
We glutted with our foemen;
The heroes and the cravens,
The spearmen and the bowmen.

We brought away from battle,
And much their land bemoaned them,
Two thousand head of cattle,
And the head of him who owned them:
Ednyfed, king of Dyfed,
His head was borne before us;
His wine and beasts supplied our feasts,
And his overthrow, our chorus.

Thomas Love Peacock

On the Late Massacre in Piedmont

Avenge, O Lord, thy slaughtered saints, whose bones
  Lie scattered on the Alpine mountains cold,
  Even them who kept thy truth so pure of old
  When all our fathers worshipped stocks and stones,
Forget not; in thy book record their groans
  Who were thy sheep, and in their ancient fold
  Slain by the bloody Piedmontese that rolled
  Mother with infant down the rocks. Their moans
The vales redoubled to the hills, and they
  To heaven. Their martyred blood and ashes sow
  O'er all the Italian fields, where still doth sway
The triple tyrant, that from these may grow
  A hundredfold, who, having learnt thy way,
  Early may fly the Babylonian woe.

John Milton

On the Massacre of Glencoe

'O tell me, Harper, wherefore flow
Thy wayward notes of wail and woe,
Far down the desert of Glencoe,
  Where none may list their melody?
Say, harp'st thou to the mists that fly,
Or to the dun-deer glancing by,
Or to the eagle, that from high
  Screams chorus to thy minstrelsy?' –

'No, not to these, for they have rest, –
The mist-wreath has the mountain-crest,
The stag his lair, the erne her nest,
  Abode of lone security.
But those for whom I pour the lay,
Not wild-wood deep, nor mountain gray,
Not this deep dell, that shrouds from day,
  Could screen from treach'rous cruelty.

'Their flag was furl'd, and mute their drum,
The very household dogs were dumb,
Unwont to bay at guests that come
  In guise of hospitality.
His blithest notes the piper plied,
Her gayest snood the maiden tied,
The dame her distaff flung aside,
  To tend her kindly housewifery.

'The hand that mingled in the meal,
At midnight drew the felon steel,
And gave the host's kind breast to feel
  Meed for his hospitality!
The friendly hearth which warm'd that hand,
At midnight arm'd it with the brand,
That bade destruction's flames expand
  Their red and fearful blazonry.

'Then woman's shriek was heard in vain,
Nor infancy's unpitied plain,
More than the warrior's groan, could gain
  Respite from ruthless butchery!
The winter wind that whistled shrill,
The snows that night that cloked the hill,
Though wild and pitiless, had still
  Far more than Southern clemency.

'Long have my harp's best notes been gone.
Few are its strings, and faint their tone,
They can but sound in desert lone
  Their gray-hair'd master's misery.
Were each gray hair a minstrel string,
Each chord should imprecations fling,
Till startled Scotland loud should ring,
  'Revenge for blood and treachery!''

Sir Walter Scott

Oh stay at home, my lad, and plough
  The land and not the sea,
And leave the soldiers at their drill,
And all about the idle hill
  Shepherd your sheep with me.

Oh stay with company and mirth
  And daylight and the air;
Too full already is the grave
Of fellows that were good and brave
  And died because they were.

A E Housman

Icarus Allsorts

'A meteorite is reported to have landed
in New England. No damage is said . . .'

A littlebit of heaven fell
From out the sky one day
It landed in the ocean
Not so very far away
The General at the radar screen
Rubbed his hands with glee
And grinning pressed the button
That started World War Three.

From every corner of the earth
Bombs began to fly
There were even missile jams
No traffic lights in the sky
In the times it takes to blow your nose
The people fell, the mushrooms rose

'House!' cried the fatlady
As the bingohall moved to various parts
of the town

'Raus!' cried the German butcher
as his shop came tumbling down

Philip was in the countinghouse
Counting out his money
The Queen was in the parlour
Eating bread and honey
When through the window
Flew a bomb
And made them go all funny
(By the way if you're wondering
What happened to the maid
Well in this particular raid

She lost more than her nose
In fact she came to a close
Or so the story goes.)

In the time it takes to draw a breath
Or eat a toadstool, instant death.

The rich
Huddled outside the doors of their fallout shelters
Like drunken carolsingers

The poor
Clutching shattered televisions
And last week's editions of T.V. Times
(but the very last)

Civil defence volunteers
With their tin hats in one hand
And their heads in the other

CND supporters
Their ban the bomb mojos beginning to rust
Have scrawled 'I told you so' in the dust.

A littlebit of heaven fell
From out the sky one day
It landed in Vermont
North-Eastern U.S.A.
The general at the radar screen
He should have got the sack
But that wouldn't bring
Three thousand million, seven hundred, and
  sixty-eight people back,
Would it?

Roger McGough

Meeting at Night

The grey sea and the long black land;
And the yellow half-moon large and low;
And the startled little waves that leap
In fiery ringlets from their sleep,
As I gain the cove with pushing prow,
And quench its speed i' the slushy sand.

Then a mile of warm sea-scented beach;
Three fields to cross till a farm appears;
A tap at the pane, the quick sharp scratch
And blue spurt of a lighted match,
And a voice less loud, through its joys and fears,
Than the two hearts beating each to each!

Robert Browning

My mistress' eyes are nothing like the sun;
Coral is far more red than her lips' red:
If snow be white, why then her breasts are dun;
If hairs be wires, black wires grow on her head.
I have seen roses damask'd, red and white,
But no such roses see I in her cheeks;
And in some perfumes is there more delight
Than in the breath that from my mistress reeks.
I love to hear her speak, yet well I know
That music hath a far more pleasing sound:
I grant I never saw a goddess go, –
My mistress, when she walks, treads on the ground:
And yet, by heaven, I think my love as rare
As any she belied with false compare.

William Shakespeare

The Prince of Love

How sweet I roamed from field to field,
   And tasted all the summer's pride,
'Till I the prince of love beheld,
   Who in the sunny beams did glide!

He showed me lilies for my hair,
   And blushing roses for my brow;
He led me through his gardens fair,
   Where all his golden pleasures grow.

With sweet May dews my wings were wet,
   And Phoebus fired my vocal rage;
He caught me in his silken net,
   And shut me in his golden cage.

He loves to sit and hear me sing,
   Then, laughing, sports and plays with me;
Then stretches out my golden wing,
   And mocks my loss of liberty.

William Blake

A Dream

Once in a dream (for once I dreamed of you)
We stood together in an open field;
Above our heads two swift-winged pigeons wheeled,
Sporting at ease and courting full in view.
When loftier still a broadening darkness flew,
Down-swooping, and a ravenous hawk revealed;
Too weak to fight, too fond to fly, they yield;
So farewell life and love and pleasures new.
Then as their plumes fell fluttering to the ground,
Their snow-white plumage flecked with crimson drops,
I wept, and thought I turned towards you to weep:
But you were gone; while rustling hedgerow tops
Bent in a wind which bore to me a sound
Of far-off piteous bleat of lambs and sheep.

Christina Rossetti

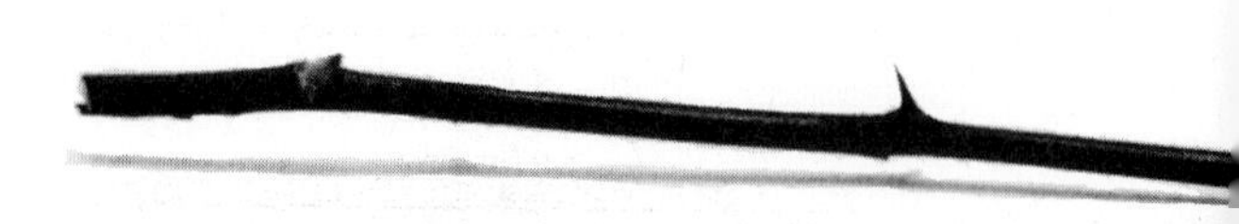

A Red, Red Rose

My love is like a red, red rose
   That's newly sprung in June:
My love is like the melody
   That's sweetly played in tune.

As fair art thou, my bonnie lass,
   So deep in love am I:
And I will love thee still, my dear,
   Till a' the seas gang dry.

Till a' the seas gang dry, my dear,
   And the rocks melt wi' the sun:
And I will love thee still, my dear,
   While the sands o' life shall run.

And fare thee weel, my only love,
   And fare thee weel a while!
And I will come again, my love,
   Thou' it were ten thousand mile.

Robert Burns

First Love

I ne'er was struck before that hour
 With love so sudden and so sweet,
Her face it bloomed like a sweet flower
 And stole my heart away complete.
My face turned pale as deadly pale,
 My legs refused to walk away,
And when she looked, what could I ail?
 My life and all seemed turned to clay.

And then my blood rushed to my face
 And took my eyesight quite away,
The trees and bushes round the place
 Seemed midnight at noonday.
I could not see a single thing,
 Words from my eyes did start –
They spoke as chords do from the string,
 And blood burnt round my heart.

Are flowers the winter's choice?
 Is love's bed always snow?
She seemed to hear my silent voice,
 Not love's appeals to know.
I never saw so sweet a face
 As that I stood before.
My heart has left its dwelling-place
 And can return no more.

John Clare

Lines

The cold earth slept below,
Above the cold sky shone;
And all around, with a chilling sound,
From caves of ice and fields of snow,
The breath of night like death did flow
Beneath the sinking moon.

The wintry hedge was black,
The green grass was not seen.
The birds did rest on the bare thorn's breast,
Whose roots, beside the pathway track,
Had bound their folds o'er many a crack,
Which the frost had made between.

Thine eyes glowed in the glare
Of the moon's dying light;
As a fenfire's beam on a sluggish stream
Gleams dimly, so the moon shone there,
And it yellowed the strings of thy raven hair,
That shook in the wind of night.

The moon made thy lips pale, beloved –
The wind made thy bosom chill –
The night did shed on thy dear head
Its frozen dew, and thou didst lie
Where the bitter breath of the naked sky
Might visit thee at will.

Percy Bysshe Shelley

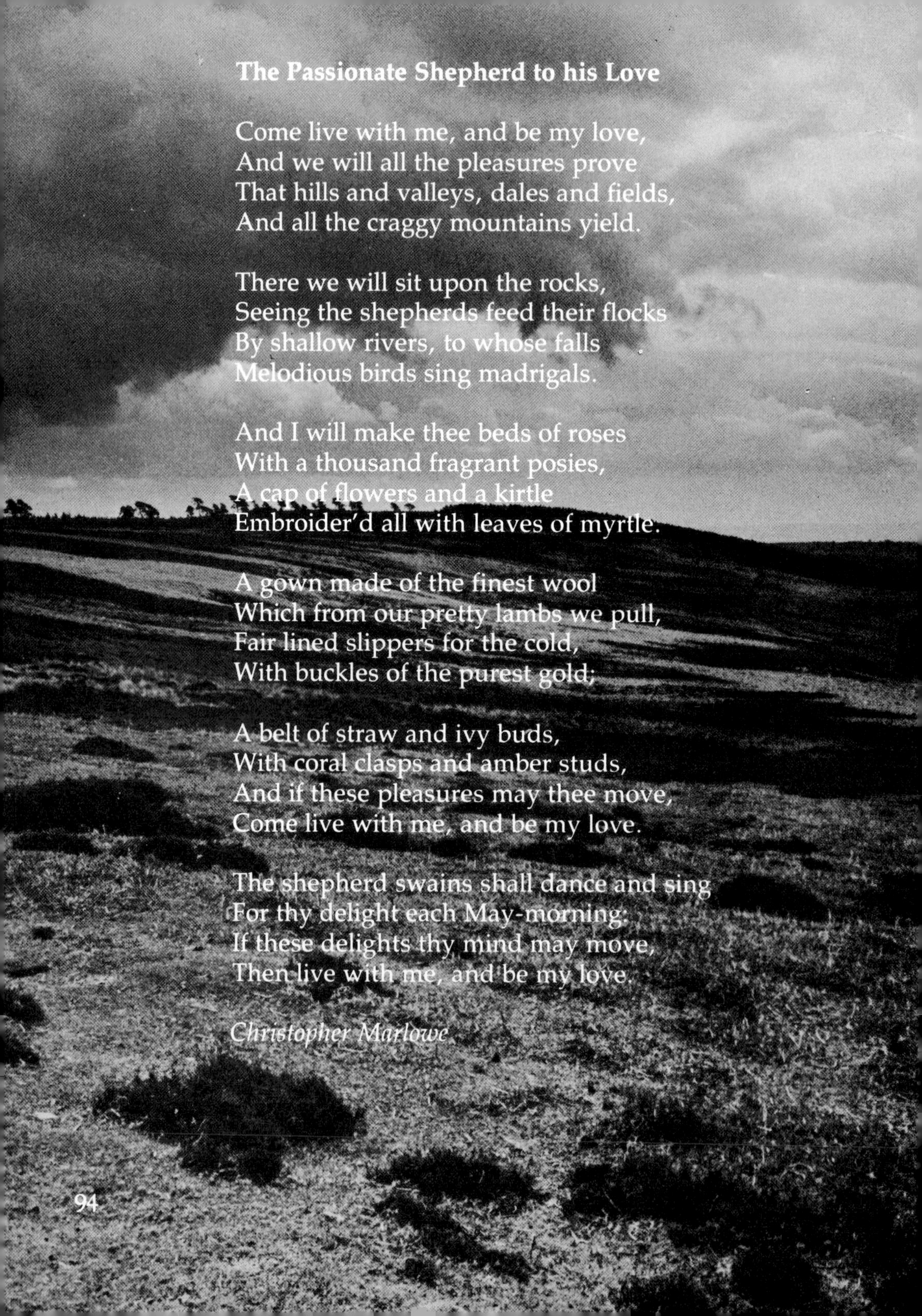

The Passionate Shepherd to his Love

Come live with me, and be my love,
And we will all the pleasures prove
That hills and valleys, dales and fields,
And all the craggy mountains yield.

There we will sit upon the rocks,
Seeing the shepherds feed their flocks
By shallow rivers, to whose falls
Melodious birds sing madrigals.

And I will make thee beds of roses
With a thousand fragrant posies,
A cap of flowers and a kirtle
Embroider'd all with leaves of myrtle.

A gown made of the finest wool
Which from our pretty lambs we pull,
Fair lined slippers for the cold,
With buckles of the purest gold;

A belt of straw and ivy buds,
With coral clasps and amber studs,
And if these pleasures may thee move,
Come live with me, and be my love.

The shepherd swains shall dance and sing
For thy delight each May-morning:
If these delights thy mind may move,
Then live with me, and be my love.

Christopher Marlowe

Come Live with Me

He. Come live with me and we'll be drovers;
When stars are lambing in the rivers,
By couples we will count the sheep
Yet kiss before we go to sleep.

All summer down the Lachlan-side
We'll sing like Clancy as we ride
Till hawks hang charmed above the plain
And shearing-time comes in again.

For love of you I'll ring the shed,
Then we'll have breakfast served in bed
By slattern maids in cotton caps,
And go to work at noon perhaps.

She. And in a basket I will keep
The skirtings of the finest sheep
For spinning tights for ballet-girls
With combs and cutters in their curls;

And they will dance at each smoke-o
For your delight upon the toe
And bring you beer and violets
In garlands for your gallon hats.

With mistletoe I'll crown my hair
And sing most sweetly to the air,
'Since Time's a shearer, where's the sin
In kissing in the super-bin?'

David Campbell

To His Coy Mistress

Had we but world enough, and time,
This coyness, Lady, were no crime.
We would sit down and think which way
To walk and pass our long love's day.
Thou by the Indian Ganges' side
Shouldst rubies find: I by the tide
Of Humber would complain. I would
Love you ten years before the Flood,
And you should, if you please, refuse
Till the conversion of the Jews.
My vegetable love should grow
Vaster than empires, and more slow;
An hundred years should go to praise
Thine eyes and on thy forehead gaze;
Two hundred to adore each breast;
But thirty thousand to the rest;
An age at least to every part,
And the last age should show your heart;
For, Lady, you deserve this state,
Nor would I love at lower rate.
  But at my back I always hear
Time's wingèd chariot hurrying near;
And yonder all before us lie
Deserts of vast eternity.
Thy beauty shall no more be found,
Nor, in thy marble vault, shall sound
My echoing song: then worms shall try
That long preserved virginity,
And your quaint honour turn to dust,
And into ashes all my lust:
The grave's a fine and private place,
But none, I think, do there embrace.

Now therefore, while the youthful hue
Sits on thy skin like morning dew,
And while thy willing soul transpires
At every pore with instant fires,
Now let us sport us while we may,
And now, like amorous birds of prey,
Rather at once our time devour
Than languish in his slow-chapt power.
Let us roll all our strength and all
Our sweetness up into one ball,
And tear our pleasures with rough strife
Thorough the iron gates of life:
Thus, though we cannot make our sun
Stand still, yet we will make him run.

Andrew Marvell

Evans

Evans? Yes, many a time
I came down his bare flight
Of stairs into the gaunt kitchen
With its wood fire, where crickets sang
Accompaniment to the black kettle's
Whine, and so into the cold
Dark to smother in the thick tide
Of night that drifted about the walls
Of his stark farm on the hill ridge.

It was not the dark filling my eyes
And mouth appalled me; not even the drip
Of rain like blood from the one tree
Weather-tortured. It was the dark
Silting the veins of that sick man
I left stranded upon the vast
And lonely shore of his bleak bed.

R S Thomas

Plastic Woman

What are you saying
Supermarket shopping lady
In the scarlet telephone box?
Lady with a shopping bag
Full of labelled pollution with secret codes
What are you saying?
Is this your dream booth?
Are you telling some plastic operator
You are Princess Grace
And can he put you through
to Buckingham Palace?
Two decimal pence
Is very little to pay for a dream in Catford.
If only the label on the door didn't say
'Out of Order'.
Shouldn't it be on you?

Spike Milligan

Upstream

I often go back
to my little song,
and hum it patiently
at my fishing-hole on the ice.
Again and again,
I hum that simple little song.
I, who all too soon
get weary when I fish,
watchfully angling,
trying to tempt
the blue-black salmon with their glossy scales,
who swim,
    upstream.

Blowingly cold, my vigil on the ice.
I soon give up
When I get home with insufficient catch
I say it was the fish that failed,
    upstream.

Yet it's wonderful to roam
the snow-soft river-ice,
as long as I support myself,
    upstream.

But now my life has slid
far from the height of the mountain-tops,
deep into the valley of old age,
    upstream.

If I hunt on land,
or try to fish,
it isn't long
before I'm sinking to my knees,
stricken with weariness,
    upstream.

I'll never feel
the surge of strength I used to get,
when I hunt inland
for my hut and those I feed,
    upstream.

I'm just a worn-out hunter now,
who'll never breathe
the great winds of the hunting-grounds again.

Yet my body's still alive
and my stomach still craves
feasts of meat.

My manhood is reduced:
an unblest fisherman,
who makes his hole
in sea or river ice,
where no trout bite,
    upstream.

Yet life is full
of interest and excitement!
I only . . .
I only have my song,
though it too glides away from me,
    upstream.

For I'm just an ordinary hunter
who never inherited singing
from the bird-song of the sky.

Ikinilik

The Astigmatic

At seven the sun that lit my world blew out
Leaving me only mist. Through which I probed
My way to school, guessed wildly at the sums
Whose marks on the board I couldn't even see.

They wanted to send me away to a special school.
I refused, and coped as best I could with half
The light lost in the mist, screwing my tears
Into my work, my gritted teeth, my writing –

Which crawled along and writhed. Think thoughts at will,
None of it comes across. Even now friends ask
'How do you read that scrawl?' The fact is, I don't;
Nobody could. I guess. But how would you

Like my world where parallels actually join,
Perspectives vary at sight? Once in a pub
I walked towards a sign marked gents over
A grating and crashed through the floor –

Well, it looked all right to me. Those steep stairs
People told me of later flattened to lines
In my half-world. The rest imagination
Supplied: when you've half a line you extend it.

The lenses drag their framework down my nose.
I still can't look strangers in the face,
Wilting behind a wall of glass at them.
It makes me look shifty at interviews.

I wake up with a headache, chew all day
Aspirins, go to bed dispirited,
Still with a dull pain somewhere in my skull,
And sleep. Then, in my dreams, the sun comes out.

Philip Hobsbaum

Who?

Who is that child I see wandering, wandering
Down by the side of the quivering stream?
Why does he seem not to hear, though I call to him?
Where does he come from, and what is his name?

Why do I see him at sunrise and sunset
Taking, in old-fashioned clothes, the same track?
Why, when he walks, does he cast not a shadow
Though the sun rises and falls at his back?

Why does the dust lie so thick on the hedgerow
By the great field where a horse pulls the plough?
Why do I see only meadows, where houses
Stand in a line by the riverside now?

Why does he move like a wraith by the water,
Soft as the thistledown on the breeze blown?
When I draw near him so that I may hear him,
Why does he say that his name is my own?

Charles Causley

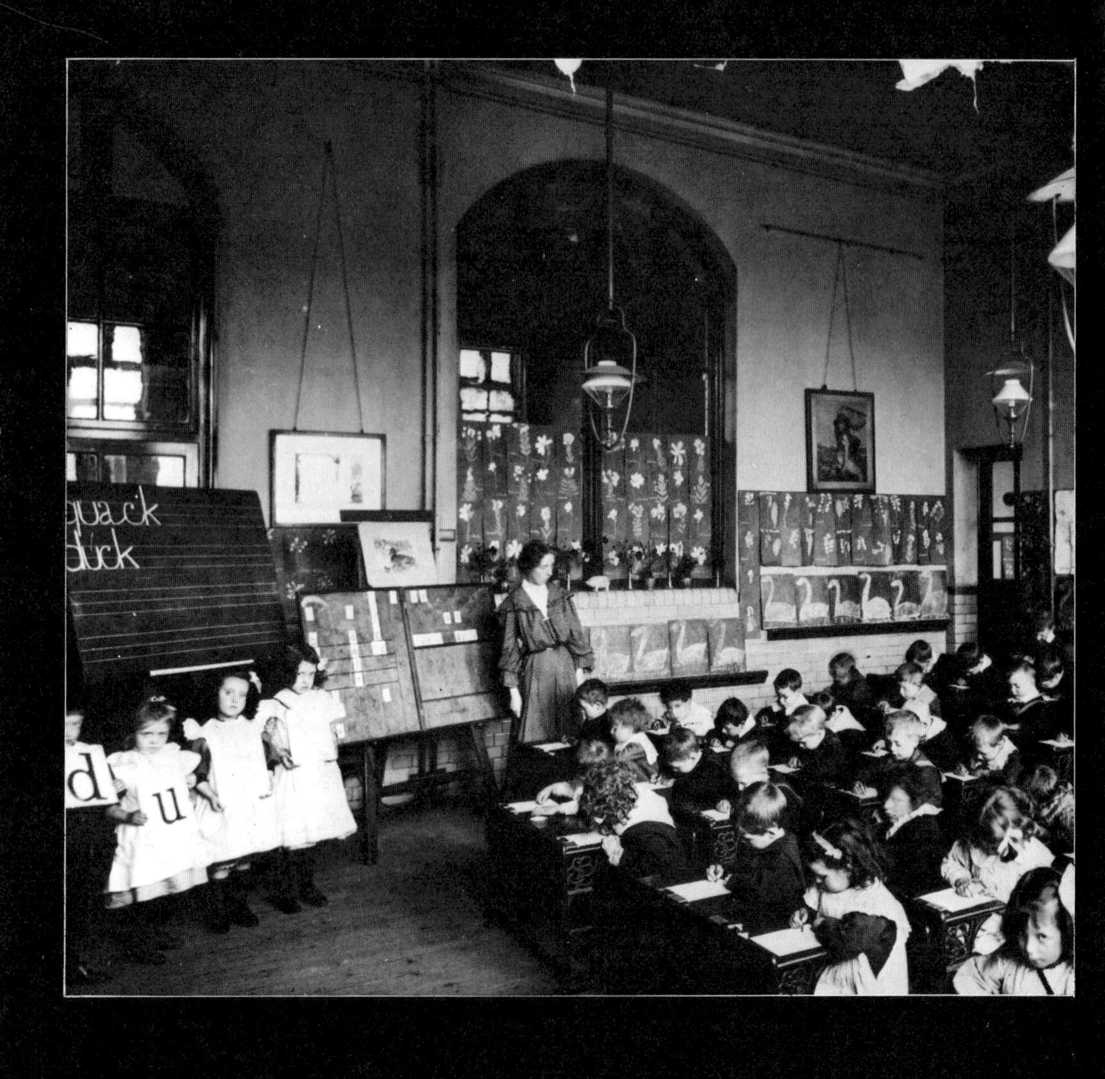
quack
duck
d
u

Schoolmistress (Miss Humm)

Straight-backed as a Windsor chair
She stood on the top playground step
And surveyed her Saturnalian kingdom.
At 8.45 precisely, she stiffened
(If that were possible), produced a key
– A large, cold dungeon-key –
Placed it below her lip, and blew.
No summons from Heaven itself
(It was a church school) was more imperious!
No angel trumpet or Mosean thunder-clap
Calling the Israelites to doom or repentance
Met swifter obedience. No Gorgon
Suspended life with such efficiency.
In the middle of a shout, a scream,
We halted. Our faces froze.
No longer George or Tom or Mary,
But forty reproductions of a single child,
Chilled to conformity. We gathered
Like captive troops and, climbing steps,
Received the inspection of her cool eyes,
Willing them away from unwashed necks
Or black-ringed fingernails,
But knowing our very thoughts were visible
If she chose to see. Nothing escaped her.
She was (as I said, a church school)
God, St Michael, the Recording Angel
And, in our guiltier moments, Lucifer –
A Lucifer in long tweed skirts
And a blouse severely fastened at the neck
By a round cameo that was no ornament
But the outward sign of inward authority.
Even the Rector, when he stepped inside
And the brown walls rumbled to his voice,
Dwindled to a curate . . .
It would have astonished us to learn, I think,
That she ate supper, went to bed,
And even, perhaps, on occasions, slept.

Clive Sansom

An Elementary School Class Room in a Slum

Far far from gusty waves, these children's faces.
Like rootless weeds the torn hair round their paleness.
The tall girl with her weighed-down head. The paper-
Seeming boy with rat's eyes. The stunted unlucky heir
Of twisted bones, reciting a father's gnarled disease,
His lesson from his desk. At back of the dim class,
One unnoted, sweet and young: His eyes live in a
  dream
Of squirrels' game, in tree room, other than this.

On sour cream walls, donations. Shakespeare's head
Cloudless at dawn, civilized dome riding all cities.
Belled, flowery, Tyrolese valley. Open-handed map
Awarding the world its world. And yet, for these
Children, these windows, not this world, are world,
Where all their future's painted with a fog,
A narrow street sealed in with a lead sky,
Far far from rivers, capes, and stars of words.

Surely Shakespeare is wicked, the map a bad example
With ships and sun and love tempting them to steal –
For lives that slyly turn in their cramped holes
From fog to endless night? On their slag heap, these
  children
Wear skins peeped through by bones and spectacles of
  steel
With mended glass, like bottle bits on stones.
All of their time and space are foggy slum
So blot their maps with slums as big as doom.

Unless, governor, teacher, inspector, visitor,
This map becomes their window and these windows
That open on their lives like crouching tombs
Break, O break open, till they break the town
And show the children to the fields and all their world
Azure on their sands, to let their tongues
Run naked into books, the white and green leaves
open
The history theirs whose language is the sun.

Stephen Spender

You'd better believe him

A fable

Discovered an old rocking-horse in Woolworth's,
He tried to feed it but without much luck
So he stroked it, had a long conversation about
The trees it came from, the attics it had visited.
Tried to take it out then
But the store detective he
Called the store manager who
Called the police who in court next morning said
'He acted strangely when arrested,
His statement read simply "I believe in
rocking-horses".
We have reason to believe him mad.'
'Quite so,' said the prosecution,
'Bring in the rocking-horse as evidence.'
'I'm afraid it's escaped sir,' said the store manager,
'Left a hoof-print as evidence
On the skull of the store detective.'
'Quite so,' said the prosecution, fearful
of the neighing
Out in the corridor.

Brian Patten

Good Taste

Travelling, a man met a tiger, so . . .
He ran. The tiger ran after him
Thinking: How fast I run . . . But

The road thought: How long I am . . . Then
They came to a cliff, yes, the man
Grabbed at an ash root and swung down

Over its edge. Above his knuckles, the tiger.
At the foot of the cliff, its mate. Two mice,
One black, one white, began to gnaw the root.

And by the traveller's head grew one
Juicy strawberry, so . . . hugging the root
The man reached out and plucked the fruit.

How sweet it tasted!

Christopher Logue

There is no Frigate like a Book
To take us Lands away
Nor any Coursers like a Page
Of prancing Poetry –
This Traverse may the poorest take
Without oppress of Toll –
How frugal is the Chariot
That bears the Human soul.

Emily Dickinson

A Brown Paper Carrierbag

IN THE TIME . . .

a spider's web woven across
the plateglass window shivers snaps
and sends a shimmering haze of lethal stars
across the crowded restaurant

IN THE TIME IT TAKES . . .

jigsaw pieces of shrapnel
glide gently towards children
tucking in   to the warm flesh
a terrible hunger sated

IN THE TIME IT TAKES TO PUT DOWN . . .

on the pavement
people come apart   slowly
at first
only the dead not screaming

IN THE TIME IT TAKES TO PUT DOWN
A BROWN PAPER CARRIERBAG.

Roger McGough

New Members Welcome

Pull the blinds
  on your emotions
Switch off your face.
Put your love into neutral
This way to the human race.

Spike Milligan

The Qualification

wurk aw yir life
nuthnty show
pit oanthi nyuze
same awl drivl

yoonyin bashn
wurkir bashn
lord this
sir soan soa thaht

shood hearma boay
sayzwi need gunz
an armd revalooshn
nuthn else wurks

awright fur him thoa
uppit thi yooni
tok aw yi like therr
thats whit its fur

Tom Leonard

The Future

The young boy stood looking up the road
to the future. In the distance both sides
appeared to converge together. 'That
is due to perspective, when you reach
there the road is as wide as it is here',
said an old wise man. The young
boy set off on the road, but,
as he went on, both sides of the
road converged until he could
go no further. He returned to ask
the old man what to do, but
the old man was dead.

Spike Milligan

The Hangman at Home

What does the hangman think about
When he goes home at night from work?
When he sits down with his wife and
Children for a cup of coffee and a
Plate of ham and eggs, do they ask
Him if it was a good day's work
And everything went well or do they
Stay off some topics and talk about
The weather, baseball, politics
And the comic strips in the papers
And the movies? Do they look at his
Hands when he reaches for the coffee
Or the ham and eggs? If the little
Ones say, Daddy, play horse, here's
A rope – does he answer like a joke:
I seen enough rope for today?
Or does his face light up like a
Bonfire of joy and does he say:
It's a good and dandy world we live
In. And if a white face moon looks
In through a window where a baby girl
Sleeps and the moon-gleams mix with
Baby ears and baby hair – the hangman –
How does he act then? It must be easy
For him. Anything is easy for a hangman,
I guess.

Carl Sandburg

On moonlit heath and lonesome bank
  The sheep beside me graze;
And yon the gallows used to clank
  Fast by the four cross ways.

A careless shepherd once would keep
  The flocks by moonlight there,
And high amongst the glimmering sheep
  The dead man stood on air.

They hang us now in Shrewsbury jail:
  The whistles blow forlorn,
And trains all night groan on the rail
  To men that die at morn.

There sleeps in Shrewsbury jail to-night.
  Or wakes, as may betide,
A better lad, if things went right,
  Than most that sleep outside.

And naked to the hangman's noose
  The morning clocks will ring
A neck God make for other use
  Than strangling in a string.

And sharp the link of life will snap,
  And dead on air will stand
Heels that held up as straight a chap
  As treads upon the land.

So here I'll watch the night and wait
  To see the morning shine,
When he will hear the stroke of eight
  And not the stroke of nine;

And wish my friend as sound a sleep
  As lads I did not know,
That shepherded the moonlit sheep
  A hundred years ago.

A E Housman

Rizpah

Wailing, wailing, wailing, the wind over land and sea –
And Willy's voice in the wind, 'O mother, come out to me.'
Why should he call me to-night, when he knows that I cannot go?
For the downs are as bright as day, and the full moon stares at the snow.

We should be seen, my dear; they would spy us out of the town.
The loud black nights for us, and the storm rushing over the down,
When I cannot see my own hand, but am led by the creak of the chain,
And grovel and grope for my son till I find myself drenched with the rain.

Anything fallen again? nay – what was there left to fall?
I have taken them home, I have number'd the bones, I have hidden them all.
What am I saying? and what are *you*? do you come as a spy?
Falls? what falls? who knows? As the tree falls so must it lie.

Who let her in? how long has she been? you – what have you heard?
Why did you sit so quiet? you never have spoken a word.
O – to pray with me – yes – a lady – none of their spies –
But the night has crept into my heart, and begun to darken my eyes.

Ah – you, that have lived so soft, what should *you* know of the night,
The blast and the burning shame and the bitter frost and the fright?
I have done it, while you were asleep – you were only made for the day.
I have gather'd my baby together – and now you may go your way.

Nay – for it's kind of you, Madam, to sit by an old dying wife.
But say nothing hard of my boy, I have only an hour of life.
I kiss'd my boy in the prison, before he went out to die.
'They dared me to do it,' he said, and he never has told me a lie.
I whipt him for robbing an orchard once when he was but a child –
'The farmer dared me to do it,' he said; he was always so wild –
And idle – and he couldn't be idle – my Willy – he never could rest.
The King should have made him a soldier, he would have been one of his best.

But he lived with a lot of wild mates, and they never would let him be good;
They swore that he dare not rob the mail, and he swore that he would;
And he took no life; but he took one purse, and when all was done
He flung it among his fellows – I'll none of it, said my son.

I came into court to the Judge and the lawyers. I told them my tale,

God's own truth – but they kill'd him, they kill'd him for robbing the mail.
They hang'd him in chains for a show – we had always borne a good name –
To be hang'd for a thief – and then put away – isn't that enough shame?
Dust to dust – low down – let us hide! but they set him so high
That all the ships of the world could stare at him, passing by.
God 'ill pardon the hell-black, raven and horrible fowls of the air,
But not the black heart of the lawyer who kill'd him and hang'd him there.

And the jailer forced me away. I had bid him my last goodbye;
They had fasten'd the door of his cell. 'O mother!' I heard him cry.
I couldn't get back tho' I tried, he had something further to say,
And now I never shall know it. The jailer forced me away.

Then since I couldn't but hear that cry of my boy that was dead,
They seized me and shut me up: they fasten'd me down on my bed.
'Mother, O mother!' – he call'd in the dark to me year after year –
They beat me for that, they beat me – you know that I couldn't but hear;
And then at the last they found I had grown so stupid and still
They let me abroad again – but the creatures had worked their will.

Flesh of my flesh was gone, but bone of my bone was left –

I stole them all from the lawyers – and you, will
  you call it a theft? –
My baby, the bones that had suck'd me, the
  bones that had laughed and had cried –
Theirs? O no! they are mine – not theirs – they
  had moved in my side.

Do you think I was scared by the bones? I kiss'd
  em, I buried 'em all –
I can't dig deep, I am old – in the night by the
  churchyard wall.
My Willy 'ill rise up whole when the trumpet of
  judgment 'ill sound,
But I charge you never to say that I laid him in
  holy ground.

And if *he* be lost – but to save *my* soul, that is all
  your desire:
Do you think that I care for *my* soul if my boy be
  gone to the fire?
I have been with God in the dark – go, go, you
  may leave me alone –
You never have borne a child – you are just as
  hard as a stone.

Madam, I beg your pardon! I think that you mean
  to be kind,
But I cannot hear what you say for my Willy's
  voice in the wind –
The snow and the sky so bright – he used but to
  call in the dark,
And he calls to me now from the church and not
  from the gibbet – for hark!
Nay – you can hear it yourself – it is coming –
  shaking the walls –
Willy – the moon's in a cloud – Goodnight. I am
  going. He calls.

Alfred, Lord Tennyson

Haunted

Evening was in the wood, louring with storm.
A time of drought had sucked the weedy pool
And baked the channels; birds had done with song.
Thirst was a dream of fountains in the moon,
Or willow-music blown across the water
Leisurely sliding on by weir and mill.

Uneasy was the man who wandered, brooding,
His face a little whiter than the dusk.
A drone of sultry wings flicker'd in his head.
The end of sunset burning thro' the boughs
Died in a smear of red; exhausted hours
Cumber'd, and ugly sorrows hemmed him in.

He thought: 'Somewhere there's thunder,' as he
strove
To shake off dread; he dared not look behind him,
But stood, the sweat of horror on his face.

He blunder'd down a path, trampling on thistles,
In sudden race to leave the ghostly trees.
And: 'Soon I'll be in open fields,' he thought,
And half remembered starlight on the meadows,
Scent of mown grass and voices of tired men,
Fading along the field-paths; home and sleep
And cool-swept upland spaces, whispering leaves,
And far off the long churring night-jar's note.
But something in the wood, trying to daunt him,
Led him confused in circles through the thicket.
He was forgetting his old wretched folly,
And freedom was his need; his throat was choking.
Barbed brambles gripped and clawed him round his
legs,
And he floundered over snags and hidden stumps.
Mumbling: 'I will get out! I must get out!'
Butting and thrusting up the baffling gloom,
Pausing to listen in a space 'twixt thorns,
He peers around with peering, frantic eyes.

An evil creature in the twilight looping,
Flapped blindly in his face. Beating it off,
He screeched in terror, and straightway something
clambered
Heavily from an oak, and dropped, bent double,
To shamble at him zigzag, squat and bestial.

Headlong he charges down the wood, and falls
With roaring brain – agony – the snap't spark –
And blots of green and purple in his eyes.
Then the slow fingers groping on his neck,
And at his heart the strangling clasp of death.

Siegfried Sassoon

Now the hungry lion roars,
And the wolf behowls the moon;
Whilst the heavy ploughman snores,
All with weary task fordone,
Now the wasted brands do glow,
Whilst the screech-owl, screeching loud,
Puts the wretch that lies in woe
In remembrance of a shroud.
Now it is the time of night
That the graves, all gaping wide,
Every one lets forth his sprite,
In the church-way paths to glide:
And we fairies, that do run
By the triple Hecate's team,
From the presence of the sun,
Following darkness like a dream,
Now are frolic; not a mouse
Shall disturb this hallow'd house;
I am sent with broom before,
To sweep the dust behind the door.

William Shakespeare

The Witches' Charm

The owl is abroad, the bat, and the toad,
And so is the cat-a-mountain;
The ant and the mole sit both in a hole,
And frog peeps out o'the fountain;
The dogs they do bay, and the timbrels play,
The spindle is now a-turning;
The moon it is red, and the stars are fled,
But all the sky is a-burning:
The ditch is made, and our nails the spade,
With pictures full, of wax and of wool;
Their livers I stick with needles quick:
There lacks but the blood to make up the flood.

Ben Jonson

Pegasus

From the blood of Medusa
Pegasus sprang.
His hoof of heaven
Like melody rang.
His whinny was sweeter
Than Orpheus' lyre,
The wing on his shoulder
Was brighter than fire.

His tail was a fountain,
His nostrils were caves,
His mane and his forelock
Were musical waves,
He neighed like a trumpet,
He cooed like a dove,
He was stronger than terror
And swifter than love.

He could not be captured,
He could not be bought,
His rhythm was running,
His standing was thought.
With one eye on sorrow
And one eye on mirth
He galloped in heaven
And gambolled on earth.

And only the poet
With wings to his brain
Can mount him and ride him
Without any rein,
The stallion of heaven
The steed of the skies,
The horse of the singer
Who sings as he flies.

Eleanor Farjeon

The Man in the Bowler Hat

I am the unnoticed, the unnoticeable man:
The man who sat on your right in the morning train:
The man you looked through like a windowpane:
The man who was the colour of the carriage, the colour
of the mounting
Morning pipe smoke.

I am the man too busy with living to live,
Too hurried and worried to see and smell and touch:
The man who is patient too long and obeys too much
And wishes too softly and seldom.

I am the man they call the nation's backbone,
Who am boneless – playable catgut, pliable clay:
The Man they label Little lest one day
I dare to grow.

I am the rails on which the moment passes,
The megaphone for many words and voices:
I am graph, diagram,
Composite face.

I am the led, the easily-fed,
The tool, the not-quite fool,
The would-be-safe-and-sound,
The uncomplaining bound,
The dust fine-ground,
Stone-for-a-statue waveworn pebble-round.

A S J Tessimond

Simplify me when I'm Dead

Remember me when I am dead
and simplify me when I'm dead.

As the processes of earth
strip off the colour and the skin:
take the brown hair and blue eye

and leave me simpler than at birth,
when hairless I came howling in
as the moon entered the cold sky.

Of my skeleton perhaps,
so stripped, a learned man will say
'He was of such a type and intelligence,' no more.

Thus when in a year collapse
particular memories, you may
deduce, from the long pain I bore

the opinions I held, who was my foe
and what I left, even my appearance
but incidents will be no guide.

Time's wrong-way telescope will show
a minute man ten years hence
and by distance simplified.

Through that lens see if I seem
substance or nothing: of the world
deserving mention or charitable oblivion,

not by momentary spleen
or love into decision hurled,
leisurely arrive at an opinion.

Remember me when I am dead
and simplify me when I'm dead.

Keith Douglas

□ indicates that the poem is recorded on the cassette (isbn 091 840315·1).
□□ recorded by the poet himself.

A Teacher's page is in four sections:

Section 1 has comments for the teacher about the poem: it explains why the poem is included where it is and highlights which of the four approaches is intended as the main one. The language in this section is geared to the teacher.

Section 2 consists of questions for the class. Some or all of these may be used for discussion or as the basis for written answers. The language in this section is geared to the child.

Section 3, where it appears, contains comments on the rhyme and rhythm/metre of the poem and/or on the figurative language used; this is in language geared to the teacher. It may also include some questions on these technical sides to the poetry, in language geared to the child. These questions are printed in italics, and the section is marked off on the page by heavy rules.

Section 4 contains follow-up work, with cross-references to other poems in the book and to other anthologies (*V* = *Voices*; *NDBV* = *New Dragon Book of Verse*).

All the anthologies mentioned are available in paperback. The three volumes of *Voices* are referred to regularly: these are, we feel, books which all children should have the opportunity to meet.

Limericks anthology pages 6–7

Limericks use a clear and well-known **pattern** of rhythm and rhyme to make them memorable. Because this pattern is well-known, variations from it can be the joke in the limerick. The Old Man from Nantucket and the Young Man from Japan are different ways of doing this. This variation within an expected pattern is very important in poetry (sometimes called **foregrounding** – see Introduction page x).
Beware: most limericks are obscene, and your pupils probably know plenty of them.

Make up (polite) limericks on yourself and your friends.

Collect limericks for a programme called, 'Around the World in – Limericks.' (e.g. Japan)

What is the regular pattern of a limerick?

Which limerick doesn't fit into this pattern? Why doesn't it?

By breaking the *expected pattern* the last limerick makes a joke. A similar kind of joke is made with the rhymes in another limerick. *Which limerick do you think makes an unexpected joke with its rhymes?* (Expected answer: Nan tucket; compare with the joking Streatham rhymes.)
Limericks have a regular **rhyme-scheme** of AABBA and a regular pattern of beats or stresses in the lines of 3:3:2:2:3. It is the regularity of the pattern which makes them so satisfying.

Study the limericks and find the rhyme scheme and the beats in the lines which make a formula for the limerick.

Good, clean, collections are:

The Blue Peter Book of Limericks Baxter and Gill (Piccolo)
The Armada Book of Limericks and
The Second Armada Book of Limericks Danby (Armada)

Epitaphs anthology pages 8–9

Our first selection of epitaphs is of short, funny ones. They rely on the convention that death is sad to heighten the joke. Their verse **pattern** gives them more bite, as the first exercise should show.

Write out some of these epitaphs without rhymes or regular rhythm. For example: Here lies John Brown, a Dentist. He is filling his last hole (or cavity). *Which version do you like best?*

Write a two-line epitaph on: a milkman, a pop-group, a hang-glider, a hamster, a dustbin.

The effect of most short epitaphs is in the *rhyming couplets*. Any rhythm takes second place to the rhyme and the playing with words.

More epitaphs appear on pages 42 and 45.

I went to the doctor, yes anthology pages 10–11

This poem relies heavily on puns for its humour. Underlying the humour is a serious comment. Thus its **feelings** are mixed.

What sort of person might be talking to the doctor?

What part of the poem do you like best?

Do you share any of the feelings of the patient?

Is the poem in any way serious?

In your group (or with whatever form of classroom organization you have) practise reading this poem to get the maximum effect from it.

Some of the puns in this poem rely on **dead metaphors** for their effect, for example: traffic jam, zebra crossing. In the next poem, *Here is the News*, notice the 'straight' use of words that were once used metaphorically: eyewitness, dawn broke, facing, held for questioning, released.

□□ **Here is the News** anthology pages 12–13

This poem satirizes the manic trivialization of news broadcasts. It needs to be read breathlessly. Again, there are surface jokes with underlying **feelings** of social comment. Note how cliché expressions are used to comic effect. As with most jokes, over-analysis can totally spoil the effect.

What different kinds of jokes can you find in the poem?

Is the ending feeble, or is its feebleness part of the joke?

In your group practise reading this poem to get the maximum effect from it.

The Forlorn Sea anthology pages 14–15

The Forlorn Sea, in contrast to the preceding poems, needs a quiet, almost private, reading. Our pupils may find it merely an amusing poem and we should accept this and not impose our adult disillusionment on them. Let them tell you what **feelings** are evoked and do not insist on a standard response.

What happens in this poem?

What picture do the words 'the forlorn sea' give you?

Why is it like a dream when they kiss and cuddle her?

What feelings do you get when you read or listen to this poem?

What words in the poem help to give you this feeling?

See also:

What's What V 1:53
Fafnir by Stevie Smith *NDBV*:189
The Forsaken Merman by Matthew Arnold, *NDBV*:197, has similarities with this poem.

Advice to a Knight anthology page 16

Advice to a Knight is another poem that uses legend and fairy tale to make its modern comment. It too has a surface **story** and an implied meaning. On one level it is a warning against ostentatious do-gooding, at another a warning that if you stick your neck out you'll get it cut off, and at yet another a rather cynical comment on rewards in society. How we interpret it will depend on our own experience. Pupils may be more positive than their teachers. It may be better not to unravel the poem too explicitly.

What happens in the first four verses?

What dangers is the knight warned against?

What does the Queen think about the knight?

What does the last line of the poem mean?

There is no rhyme scheme here and no regular rhythm, but the lines mostly consist of ten syllables, which gives a regular division to the lines.

With this you could read:

Jabberwocky V 1:19
The Dragon of Wantley V II:29
Saint V II:130
The Three Ravens V II:160
Cynddylan on a Tractor NDBV:135
The Cave of Despair NDBV:194
La Belle Dame Sans Merci NDBV:195
from The Passing of Arthur NDBV:203
The Lady of Shalott NDBV:204

Old English Riddle anthology page 17

In contrast to the last poem which was a modern one using myth, this is an Anglo-Saxon Riddle describing a shield, though it may be best not to reveal this too soon. Riddles rely on **images** to work.

What is being described here?

What gave you the clue? OR Why did you find this difficult?

Which parts of the poem could apply just as well to a man and which parts couldn't?

What picture of Saxon battles do you get from this poem?

More Anglo-Saxon riddles are in *V* I:7.
Other riddles: *V* I:13–16.

☐ **Goody Blake and Harry Gill** anthology pages 18–21

This **story** illustrates the value of discursiveness and repetition in poetry (despite the modern fashion for the concise lyric). The 'Advertisement' to *Lyrical Ballads* claims that the tale is 'founded on a well-authenticated fact which happened in Warwickshire'. It is particularly good for group reading aloud. (This is a slightly shortened version of the original.)

Who is Goody Blake?

Who is Harry Gill?

What is Goody Blake's crime?

How does she get her revenge?

Why, in the last two lines, are farmers told to think of Goody Blake and Harry Gill?

The first verse could be summed up in six words: Why was Harry Gill always cold? The verse actually has fifty words. Do the extra 44 words add anything?

Can you find other examples of words that aren't strictly necessary?

Do you believe that this is a true story?

Tell this story as you would naturally.

What are the main differences between the way you tell the story and the way it is written here? (Expected answers: rhyme, metre, repetition.)

What advantages are there in telling the story like this?

The next Foregrounding section is on page 140.

Look at verse 2: 'His cheeks were red as ruddy clover
His voice was like the voice of three.'
Here we are told that one thing is like another thing. Sometimes we are told in exactly what way they are alike.
Harry's 'cheeks' are like the 'clover' because they are as 'red'.
Harry's 'voice' is like 'three voices' put together (implied: the same volume *as three voices).*

There is another **simile** *in the next verse. Can you unravel it?*

When you have established what a simile is have a 'simile hunt'. *How many similes can you find in Poems 2 in x minutes?* You can be more specific and ask for ones that state explicitly what the ground of comparison is (*lonely as a cloud*) or for ones where it is implied (*he fought like a lion*).

The **rhyme scheme** is a regular ABAB. The lines have four beats each and are written in **iambic tetrameters**. The iamb will be seen through this book to be the most common metrical foot.

Look at the rhyme-scheme in the verses and pick out the beats to a line and say what all the verses have in common.

Useful follow-ups are:

The Little Cart *V* I:28
The Housewife's Lament *V* I:45
Bishop Hatto *NDBV*:128

□□ **Saturdays I put on my boots** anthology pages 22–23

This poem tells a story and evokes feelings but we can also use it to show how precise details create **images**.

What happens in this story?

How long do you think the tunnel is?

What does he mean by, 'No one said we'd left him'?

What different feelings did the narrator have on that particular Saturday?

Where in his description of the river does his imagination take over from his accurate reporting?

Which group of words gives you the best picture of the place?

Which group of words gives you the best idea of the boys' feelings when Thatcher disappeared?

This poem shows a standard use of **exaggeration** in the lines 'and screamed for hours' and 'It was miles'.

Why does he say this if it isn't true?

Can you find other examples of exaggeration?

☐☐ **The Galloping Cat** anthology pages 24–25

This is another Stevie Smith poem that needs to be read with verve (as she has recorded it herself). Here the cat's opinion of himself is quite different from our opinion of him. **Images** can be used ironically.

What happens in this poem?

Practise reading the first 10 lines to get the rhythm as interesting as possible.

What does the cat think of himself?

What does he say about himself that shows this (apart from 'galloping about doing good')?

What does the angel think of the cat?

How do you know?

Do you agree with the cat or the angel, or do you have your own opinion of him?

Read the poem aloud to show the cat's indignation.

This poem can be used to introduce the idea of **irony**: the author's real view of the cat is quite different from the words she puts in the cat's mouth.

Glasgow October 1972 anthology page 26
Milk for the Cat anthology pages 27–28

This group of poems about animals starts with two which have clear **images** of cats drinking milk, although in very different circumstances. *Milk for the Cat* shows especially how images convey feelings.

First poem:
What exactly is happening in this poem?
Who is going to win?
What is Sarah's attitude to the contest?
Why is Tiny said to be kittening through his milk?
Second poem:
What is happening in this poem?
What group of words tells you most clearly that this cat likes milk?
How do the feelings of the cat change?
What words tell you most clearly about the different feelings she has?
Which poem gives you the best picture of cats drinking milk?
Which poem do you like best?
How would you read the poems to give the best effect?

Milk for the Cat relies heavily on **exaggeration** for its effect.
What parts of this poem aren't literally true?
Do you find that they help you to get a picture of the cat in your mind?
Do any of them seem to you to be too *exaggerated?*

Other cat poems:
Christopher Smart Considers his Cat, Jeoffry *V* I:88
Cat-Goddesses *V* III:84
Cats no less Liquid than their Shadows *NDBV*:81
Macavity: the Mystery Cat *NDBV*:82
A Cat *NDBV*:83

A Widow Bird anthology page 29

A Widow Bird makes its emotional mood explicit in the first line and then uses **images** in the next 7 to create the same feelings in the reader.

Does each line after the first have a sad picture?

Which line do you like best?

Which one goes best with the picture of the bird?

If the first line read, 'A bird sat' would you still get the same sad feelings?

Another dead bird:
Death of a Bird V I:98

Fetching Cows anthology page 30

Fetching Cows is full of **images** creating a mood. (Does it work only for those who already know the scene?). You may need to draw a picture to explain why the haycart is prickeared.

Which words tell you what time of year this is?

Which words tell you what time of day this is?

Which words give you the best picture of the cows?

Why does he say, 'Hay breath and milk breath'?

Why is the sun like a ship?

What mood does this poem suggest to you?

What words in particular help to create this mood?

Look at the end of the second verse. Is there anything surprising in its last line? (Expected answer: a soft nose being compared with something as hard as coal)

Do you think a cow's muzzle is as 'shiny' as wet coal?

If I say the word 'coal' to you, what do you think of?

In these sections (pages 127 and 134) we have looked at three examples of what is called Foregrounding (see introduction p. x):

1 something is unexpected, like an unusually long last line

2 something is unusually regular and repetitive

3 a comparison is unusual because we don't usually think of the things together.

Writing in an unexpected way catches the reader's attention.

Metaphor can be approached first as simile without the *like* or *as*.

Look at the last two lines.

Where could you put the word 'like'?

Is there any advantage in leaving it out?

What other metaphors can you find in this poem?

Another cow poem:

Bags of Meat *V* II:62

The Spider anthology page 31
The Wind begun to rock the Grass anthology page 32

First poem:
This poem and the last one evoke **feelings** of sadness through their images which treat the creatures as if they were human. How far does this help our observation or widen our sympathies? You may need to explain 'yarn' and 'tapestries'.

Three groups of words suggest the invisibility of a new spider's web (unperceived Hands, from Nought to Nought, unsubstantial Trade). Which do you like best?

What is the spider quicker than us at?

What quick remedy does the housewife have?

Second poem:
This poem on wind develops the personification in *The Spider* and *A Widow Bird* through its **images**.

What are the stages in the storm?

Why does she say the wind 'rocks' the grass?

Why does she say leaves are 'unhooked'?

In what way can the thunder be said to have 'hurried slow'?

Which picture of the storm do you like best?

This poem provides a good introduction to **personification**.
What things are being compared to persons?
When you have established what personification is try a 'personification hunt'.

In both poems Emily Dickinson writes in **iambic metre** in alternate tetrameter/trimeter.

Child on Top of a Greenhouse anthology page 33

In *Child on Top of a Greenhouse* there are precisely observed details contributing to the **feeling** of exhilaration. Each line has a different picture, making this a good model for imitation.

What feeling does the child have?

How do you know?

Does each line help to build up the same feeling?

Which do you like best?

Is 'billowing' a dead, dying, or living **metaphor**? *(originally from the billows of the sea)*
Compare with 'plunging' and 'tossing': are these dead or still living?

Wind is a popular subject for poets and/or anthologists:

Winter Gales *V* I:129
Wild Iron *V* I:132
The Wind *V* II:134
Night Wind *V* II:136
The Bird of Night *V* II:136
Fragment XXIV *V* II:137
The North Wind *V* II:137
Wind *NDBV*:13
Wenlock Edge *NDBV*:14
Wuthering Heights *NDBV*:15

Daysies anthology page 34

Daysies, along with the following poems, conveys the **feelings** aroused by the sight of flowers. Chaucer chooses the commonest and simplest of flowers and gives it importance, as well as explaining the origin of its name.

Glossary:

mede – meadow	weste – sink in the West
erst – before	shoop – arrange, plan
nam – am not	swiche – such
agein the sonne – in the sun	mot – must
morwe – morning	faire mot falle – good luck must come
shene – bright	ye – eye
ginneth – begins	

What does the poet say the daisy is like in the morning?

Where does the poet describe the evening, and what does he say the flower does then?

What does the name 'daisy' mean, according to Chaucer?

Why do you think it was given that name?

Where in the poem does Chaucer show that he likes the daisy best of all flowers?

What other flower names do you know which have a meaning related to what the flowers look like?

These lines are written in rhyming couplets and with a regular rhythm: *read 5–6 lines to yourselves and then say how many beats there are in each line.*

The regularity of **pattern**, with **rhyming couplets** and **iambic pentameters**, may also be brought out.

Compare also: *Snow Drop V* III:10

The Lily anthology page 36
The Dandelion's pallid tube anthology page 37

These two poems use **imagery** to convey sentiments about two flowers, the lily and the dandelion.

First poem:
How does Blake show it is unexpected for a rose to have a thorn or a sheep a horn?

What contrast is being made between the lily and the rose?

Why should the lily in 'Love' delight?

Second poem:
What is the 'pallid tube'?

Why does it 'astonish' the grass?

Why does Winter become 'an infinite Alas'?

In what way do you think the flower is 'shouting'?

In the last line 'sepulture' means 'being buried underground': what are the Suns and what is their Proclamation?

In connection with flowers, compare also:
The Loving Dexterity *V* III:12
The Sick Rose *NDBV*:214

Mist in the Meadows anthology page 37
The Fog anthology page 38

Pages 37 to 39 show four poets approaching the idea of Fog in different ways. The **imagery** used by each is different but they are all describing the same phenomenon. The W. H. Davies poem describes someone's **feelings** in the presence of fog rather than in the movements of the fog itself.

First poem:
What exactly is happening in the poem by Clare?
What is the fog compared to?
What feeling does the poem produce in you?

Second poem:
What effects is the fog having on the writer's face and throat – how does he feel?

In the fourth verse how do you think the street lamps, the car lights and the stars become confused? Is this very likely?

Where else in the poem does the writer say his sight of things became confused?

How could a blind man lead him home in this situation?

W. H. Davies writes 'Fog' with an ABCD **rhyme-scheme** and in regular **iambic trimeters.**

Compare Fog, Goody Blake *and* Fetching Cows *and see how they are all composed in the same rhythm but the number of beats (or feet) is different in each poem.*

The fog comes anthology page 39
November Night, Edinburgh

First poem:
In the Sandburg poem the fog is likened to a cat. In what way is it like one?

Of the four poems on fog which do you think best conveys the effects of fog?

Which of the four poems do you like most?

Can you think of anything else which might be used to describe fog, or which, like a cat, could be used to personify fog?

Second poem:
What references to fog can you find in the last poem (e.g. the brown air fumes)?

Pretending that something like fog can behave like living creatures is called **personification**. *Where is fog personified in this poem?*

How do you think the world can be 'a bear shrugged in his den'?

This pair of pages is worth coming back to when you have explored figurative language. It provides examples of **similes, metaphors, personification, exaggeration.**

For similar effects of weather and atmosphere compare:
A January Night *V* III:165
At Day-Close in November *V* III:166
Charles Dickens's *Bleak House* opens with a prose poem on fog.

Friday Morning anthology page 40

Sidney Carter has written many modern hymns and songs, telling **stories** from the Bible in ballad form; one of his best known is 'Lord of the Dance'. The **pattern** and rhythm are most important; but the irony in this song should not be missed. Read it to the class, bringing out the rhythm.

Which Friday morning was this?

Who was the carpenter?

What was the apple mentioned here?

Why does the speaker blame God? (He makes three clear accusations.)

In view of the last verse, what does the speaker not realize about the carpenter?

Rhythm and rhyme are important in songs and carols. In *Friday Morning* the rhyme-scheme is AABB (or rhyming couplets) and there are eight beats to a line but there is an obvious break half-way through each line so the beats are really 4:4; the chorus is 3:3.

How many beats are there in each line of a verse? Tap out the rhythm when you have worked it out.

Compare the subject matter of:

Jesus and his mother V III:60

The Carol of the Poor Children anthology page 41

This carol gives an original slant to the events of Christmas night. It has the regular **pattern** of a song; and there is an underlying message.

What is 'this night of nights'?

What is the 'new star'?

The singers are 'poor children': where in this song is their poverty described and where is it contrasted with rich people?

What comforts can the new king offer the poor children? Is the new king in any way poor himself?

In what way can the poor children feel closer to this new king?

Most carols describe the scene of Christ's birthplace in a straightforward 'eye-witness' way: do you know any other carols or stories which tell it through the eyes of someone unusual?

For different approaches to Bible Stories and to Christmas compare:

Darky Sunday School *V* I:43
Ballad of the Bread Man *V* III:63
How to Paint a Perfect Christmas *V* III:168
Journey of the Magi *NDBV*:225

Epitaph in Lydford Churchyard anthology page 42

Describing a person completely in terms of something else is **metaphor**, a common form of **imagery**. This epitaph is a classic example of such imagery.

What words connected with watches and watchmaking can you find in each of the three sections of this epitaph? Divide into groups and study one section each.

What is meant by people who did not know 'his key'?

Write an epitaph – shorter than this one, if you like – for one of the following, using the imagery of his occupation in the same way: teacher, astronaut, butcher, gravedigger, doctor.

Compare the following epitaphs, which also use the language of the particular occupation:

On John Spong, a Jobbing Carpenter *V* I:35
On William Braithwaite, Whitesmith *V* I:35
Epitaph on an Auctioneer *V* I:94

Song anthology page 43
The Spiritual Railway anthology page 44

First poem:
This poem on death takes an optimistic, cheerful view of dying compared with many; the **feeling** expressed is one of contentment. This should come out in discussion.

What is the speaker asking to be done at her death?

Do you feel this is a strange request?

What is she saying about death in this song?

In *Song* the **rhyme scheme** is ABCB. There is no obvious metrical foot used regularly but there are three beats discernible in each line.

Second poem:
This, like the Watchmaker's epitaph, is a good example of sustained metaphor, and will help the understanding of **image**.

Why should these lines have been written in memory of these two men in particular?

What must people do to join the Spiritual Railway?

What do you think are the 'tunnels dark and dreary'?

What is meant by 'at any station on the line'?

The Spiritual Railway is written in **rhyming couplets** and in regular **iambic tetrameters**.

Can you name the metre in which 'The Spiritual Railway' is written?

For further views on impending death, compare:
Afterwards NDBV:237

Requiem anthology page 45

Requiem *also takes a contented view of dying: why is the speaker so contented?*

What sort of person do you think is speaking and what has his occupation been?

What does the word 'grave' mean at the beginning of the second verse? Is it a good word or a strange one to use here? What different meaning of 'grave' do you know?

In *Requiem* the **rhyme** is AAAB:CCCB and there are four beats to the line.

What is the rhyme scheme and is the rhyme related between the two verses?

How many beats are there to each line?

For further epitaphs, compare:

Epitaph on a Tyrant V III:58
Reader, Pass On V II:159
Epitaph on an Army of Mercenaries: NDBV:183

Here lies a poor woman anthology page 45
An Inscription by the Sea

First poem:

The first epitaph here is a more humorous one, conveying a vivid picture of the 'poor woman'; it also has a regular **pattern** and rhythm.

The second is a simple inscription on someone whose death denied him a gravestone.

In the first poem: in line 2 was help hired or not? What sort of help is meant?

What picture do you get of the 'poor woman'? What sort of life has she had? Was she a cheerful personality?

The **rhyme-scheme** for *The poor woman* is AABB and the rhythm is dactylic. It is in **dactylic tetrameters**, but notice how the dactyls overlap from one line to the next, e.g.:

The last words she said were 'Dear friends, I am going,
Where washing an't wanted, nor mending, nor sewing.'

Read the verse to yourselves: how many beats are there to a line? Tap out the rhythm of the lines on your desk.

Second poem:

In the second epitaph: why does the dead man have no dust to cover him?

Who is the stranger?

Where did the dead man drown?

The Inscription is written in **iambic metre**, with the beats/feet going 4:3:4:3:4:4:3

For further epitaphs, compare:

The Housewife's Lament V I:45
Epitaph to the Memory of Captain Henry Clark V II:151

The Express anthology page 46

This poem uses several different **images** to convey the train, its sound and its surroundings. It contrasts with *Tremors* in that there is variety of image rather than one sustained metaphor.

Through this poem the express is compared with several different things: what different images can you find which describe the train, its sound and its movements?

What is the 'heavy page of death'? What is this sort of image called?

What is meant by 'the metre of her wheels'?

Why is the happiness 'white'?

How can speed throw up 'parallels clean like the steel of guns'?

What images of beauty are referred to in the last two lines which are often used in poetry?

For a further description of the sounds and movement of a train, compare:

Night Mail NDBV:17

and for further description of sound and movement see:

A Fire Truck V II:17

MovingAlong by Barbara Ireson is an entire anthology about travel.

For an extreme example of different images applied to one idea, see:

Thirteen Ways of looking at a Blackbird V III:155

A Local Train of Thought anthology page 47
Tremors anthology page 48

First poem:
Hearing a train in the distance produces **feelings** of familiarity, while travelling by train often arouses feelings of loneliness.

What does the train do at 'one-fifty'?

What is it about the train that comforts the poet?

Why is the warning whistle needless?

Why does he feel the train is 'quite like an old familiar friend'?

Second poem:
This poem takes a simple child's game at a railway line and uses it as an **image** of an attitude to life.

What exactly are the children doing in the first two-and-a-half verses of the poem?

What do you understand by the expression 'having an ear to the ground'? In what situations might you use the expression?

What are the tremors in verse 4?

What has become 'a matter of survival'?

What is the 'procession of explosions' which 'there can be no stopping'?

What 'end' is known?

Can you think of a different image to show how people keep looking out for the dangers in life, whenever they may appear?

For familiarity with a train, compare:
I Like to See it Lap the Miles NDBV:16

For another child's game taking on deeper significance in adult life, compare:
By St. Thomas Water NDBV:95

Midnight on the Great Western anthology page 50

Trains are often used as **images**, perhaps because train journeys are often conducive to silent thought and imagination.

First poem:

What picture do you get of the carriage and its occupants from the first two verses?

What exactly is the poet wondering about the boy, and why is he worried for him?

The last verse is made difficult by some strange word-order: line 2 means 'far above our rude realms'. What then do the first two lines mean?

'mete' means 'measure' or 'judge': what is the poet saying about the thoughts and ideas of the boy compared with his own?

In *Midnight on the Great Western* the second and fifth lines **rhyme**, but also notice the rhyming of the two halves of the fourth lines. The **rhythm** of the third and fourth lines particularly brings out the rhythm of a train.

Corner Seat anthology page 51
To a Fat Lady Seen from the Train

First poem:
Why is this poem called Corner Seat?

How is the face 'suspended in a moving night'?

Why does the reflection seem lonely?

Why do you think people often seem lonely when you see them travelling on a train?

Second poem:
What exactly is the fat lady missing?

Why are her gloves mentioned?

Why do you think 'nobody loves' her?

In 'To a Fat Lady' the **rhyme** uses just two sounds in a scheme of ABAAABAB and the **dactylic rhythm** also echoes the rhythm of a train.

□□ **Thistles** anthology pages 52–57

This group of five poems on thistles shows a variety of **images** and provides an opportunity for comparison. We suggest treating them as a group, partly for variety and partly to provide a convenient revision point. Each poem has one dominant image or idea:

□ Clare: the thistle as fearless plant
□ Young: thistledown like ghosts
□□ Lee: childhood experience of thistles
□□ Hughes: the feud – thistle v. man
□□ Stallworthy: thistles like infantry soldiers.

We suggest dividing the class into five groups, or a multiple of five groups, so that each group can consider one poem and then, when the groups share their ideas with the rest of the class, the differences of approach should emerge painlessly.

Read each poem carefully. Decide what is the main thing each writer is saying (the story).

What kind of pattern does each poem have?

What pictures do you like best in the poems?

What different feelings are there in the poems?

What order would you read them aloud in?

This section on thistles gives an opportunity to compare the way different poets use figurative language. Does each poem have one dominant **metaphor** which is developed and extended? What **similes** are used? How do the similes strengthen the extended metaphors? For example: in Ted Hughes's poem (page 56) there is a sustained metaphor of fighting, suggesting that thistles are tough and persistent. List the words and phrases that reinforce this. The word 'like' appears twice; is there any connection between the two?

John Clare writes here in **rhyming couplets** and the metre is **iambic**, in **pentameters**.

The metre of this poem is iambic: how many beats, or feet, are there to a line?

Thistles Cont.

Jon Stallworthy's 'Thistles' has an interesting **rhyme-scheme** of ABCABC.

There seem to be few other poems on thistles. They make an appearance in *The Village NDBV*:19. If you want a change from thistles try

Tall Nettles V I:113

□□ **Think of this tower-block** anthology pages 59–60

This poem is one which may be appreciated on two levels – and this is an extension of **image** where one thinks of one idea in terms of another. On the surface this is a humorous poem about tower-blocks, but underlying is a serious statement of how joyless and inhuman they are and how they can be imposed on people by those in authority.

Who is the speaker in this poem?

Why do you think he describes the tower-block as he does in lines 1–6?

In the second section there is frequent use of 'no' and 'not': why do you think this is so and what does it make you feel about tower-blocks?

Have you ever been into or lived in a tower-block? If you have, how much of this poem is true or familiar?

There are a lot of funny ideas and remarks in this poem: do you think that it is in any way a serious poem?

Read the poem out in the tone of the man who is giving the description and the instructions.

For a further view of the clinical treatment of the environment, compare:

We Are Going to See the Rabbit NDBV:85

Number 14 anthology page 63
The Hammers anthology page 63

First poem:
The simple **story** told in this poem has an underlying comment about buildings falling and rising, like *Tower-block* and *Slough*.

What is happening to the street which Number 14 is in?

What is meant by 'grew up under your father's belt'?

How is there 'each day a bit more sky'?

'Its time come and gone': what does this say about Number 14 and houses like it? Does it remind you of another earlier poem?

What will deliver 'one more stroke'?

The next two poems take different attitudes to the changes in buildings that surround us. In the first the **pattern/rhythm** contributes to the effect of the hammers (the metre is trochaic). The pattern in the second makes full use of the shortened last line to create a climax or an ironic twist to each verse and these last lines rhyme in pairs.

What is the poem Hammers *about?*

What difference is there between the 'dust and clay' in verse 1 and that in verse 2?

How many beats are there in each line? How does this add to the effect of a poem called Hammers?

Slough anthology pages 64–65

Why does the poet want bombs to fall on Slough? How could these bombs be 'friendly'?

What do you think is meant by 'tinned minds, tinned breath'?

Who is 'that man' in verse 4?

What sort of person does not 'know birdsong from the radio'?

What sort of life is being led by the young clerks and their wives?

What do you think is meant by the last two lines?

What rhyming pattern can you find in this poem?

Do you know of any town which is like this description of Slough?

Slough uses an **exaggeration** of feeling rather than exaggerated description. How effective is it? Could it be counter-productive? The poem was first published in 1937.

The Hammers has a **rhyme-scheme** of ABCCAC and is written in **trochees,** i.e. with the beat on the odd syllables. Compare the iambic rhythm, with the beat on the even syllables, of *Slough*.

Nóise of hámmers ónce I héard,

Mány hámmers, búsy hámmers

Come, fríendly bómbs, and fáll on Slóugh

It ísn't fít for húmans nów

In *Slough* the first three lines rhyme, but notice also the fourth lines of each verse rhyme in pairs.

Consider

Latter-Day Geography Lesson V II:88

Telegraph Poles anthology page 66
The Pylons anthology page 67

Telegraph Poles and *Pylons* lend themselves easily to **imagery** for the purposes of description. Here *Telegraph Poles* is one sustained metaphor while *Pylons* involves similes.

First poem:

What image or metaphor is used to describe telegraph poles here?

How many words can you find which contribute to this one image?

What is meant by rams mustering 'their horned and tenor herds'? Does 'horned' have more than one meaning here?

Second poem:

What exactly was the 'secret' of the hills?

How have the pylons spoiled that secret?

What is 'perspective'? How do pylons produce 'the quick perspective of the future'?

What is a 'trek'? How can pylons dwarf the country by their trek?

What sort of cities are the pylons dreaming of? Do you think any exist yet?

Once at Piertarvit anthology pages 68–69
Song anthology page 70

First poem:
This poem tells us an unusual but simple **story**, built around an incident which is the climax of the poem. It also expresses a variety of **feelings** experienced by the children involved.

What exactly happens in this story?

The children experience different feelings during the story: what are these feelings (e.g. contentment, shock, horror, surprise, relief) and where in the poem do the feelings change from one to another?

Where does the climax come in this poem?

How does Ian feel after the incident?

What is meant by 'The whole sky curdled
Over Piertarvit.'?

In groups plan a reading of the poem, noting where to change the pace from relaxed to stunned to bewildered. Then one person from each group read the poem out.

Second poem:
This poem also expresses **feelings**, but this time misplaced feelings rather than lack of any.

Why did the dove die?

Why is the poet surprised that it died?

What is this poem saying about keeping creatures as pets?

What is the rhyme-scheme here? Is it regular all through?
How many beats are there to a line?

Compare:
In the House V I:83
Death of a Bird V I:98
Self-Pity V II:66

Numbers anthology page 71

In *Numbers* the **imagery** of different numbers is used to make a simple point about the smallness of the individual.

Why does the first verse start with a number of over one thousand and finish with one and four?

Why do you think the poet contrasts the four windows with the one skylight?

What is the point of mentioning one seagull compared with 231 earlier?

Is this just a poem about looking through windows, or do you think it is expressing some other underlying idea?

Can you see any connection between Numbers *and* Once at Piertarvit, *apart from the obvious one that they both involve birds?*

For another treatment of the smallness of the individual, compare:

The Spider *V* II:53

The Dog Lovers anthology page 72

The Dog Lovers conveys the mixed **feelings** many people have about pets: they are fun so long as they are not inconvenient. This poem uses **irony** for its effect.

In what ways was the home 'a very good home' for the dog?

In what ways was it not a good home?

Why did the dog escape?

What does the last line say about people's attitudes to pets?

The Dog Lovers is **ironically** titled.

What would you expect to find in a poem with this title?

What would be a more accurate title?

Why is this a good title, even though it isn't very accurate?

The Dog Lovers has no rhyme scheme or metre but each line conveys a new idea and thus the line divisions contribute to the effect,

Why do you think the lines divide where they do?

Compare:

Two Songs of a Fool V I:83

My Mother saw a Dancing Bear anthology page 73

Here a story is used as an **image** to convey popular attitudes towards performing animals.

What exactly is the scene by the schoolyard?

What different tricks does the bear perform?

Why is the 'summer heat' mentioned in the second verse?

Where else is it mentioned or implied that the bear is very hot?

What is meant by 'shaming the laughter to a stop'?

Why are 'far-distant forests and the snow' mentioned at the end?

Charles Causley has written this with an ABCB **rhyme-scheme** and in **iambic tetrameters**.

What rhyme-scheme can you find in the poem?

How many beats are there in each line? Can you show how the lines are basically iambic?

For human attitudes to animals compare:

Two Performing Elephants V I:92
Horses Aboard V I:92
Auguries of Innocence NDBV:58

Song of the Battery Hen anthology page 74

This poem sets out to show the **feelings** of the battery hen and the lack of feelings of the humans involved. As with *The Dog Lovers* the chief weapon is irony, and the poet also uses contrast to highlight his point.

What is wrong or unnatural about the hen's accommodation as described in the first verse?

Why does the poet give such an accurate description of which hen is speaking in lines 1–5 of the second verse?

What do you think is meant by 'I am the one who sounds loudest in my head'?

What is a broiler house? Why does the poet say 'one cockerel grows' rather than 'crows'?

Why do you think the poem ends as it does?

We may well feel that this poem **understates** the horrors of modern chicken rearing and is more effective for it. A straight-forward description (as in *Animal Machines* by Ruth Harrison (Stuart and Watkins), 1975) could be read as a comparison. The use of 'chicken-shit' emphasizes the blandness of the rest of the poem.

Compare:

A Sheep Fair V I:93

One summer evening anthology pages 76–77

This is a **story** of an adventure, from *The Prelude* by William Wordsworth. It combines a description of his **feelings** both during and after his experience.

In what way was his setting off from the shore 'an act of stealth and troubled pleasure'?

How does the poet describe the effect of the oars and the boat's movement on the water?

How does he try to row straight?

What change takes place on the horizon?

What exactly did the poet experience with 'the peak'? What different features made the peak frightening?

What thoughts and feelings did the incident leave with the poet?

This extract from *The Prelude* is written in **blank verse**, that is in a regular rhythm but with no rhyme. The lines are **iambic pentameters.**

For another excerpt from The Prelude see *NDBV*:93.

Stanzas anthology page 78

☐ **Harp Song of the Dane Women** anthology page 79

The next four double-pages have poems on the subject of war. Although the actual events described took place in the past, the causes represented and the feelings aroused are still relevant.

Byron has mixed and rather bitter **feelings** about fighting for causes. These *Stanzas* were written in 1820 and it is worth remembering that Byron did not take a detached view but in 1823 went out to Greece to fight for the cause of Greek Independence, joining the Greek 'freedom fighters' against the Turks.

The *Harp Song of the Dane Women* comes from Rudyard Kipling's novel *Puck of Pook's Hill*, and although from fiction conveys vividly the desperate feelings of those who are left behind in war.

First poem:

What reasons does Byron offer for fighting?

What rewards does he see offered?

How serious is this poem?

The rhythm and rhyme in *Stanzas* is regular: the **rhyme-scheme** ABAB and the metre **anapaestic** with the beat/stress not coming until the third beat.

Compare: *Dulce et Decorum Est* *NDBV*:180

Second poem:

What is 'the old grey Widow-maker'?

What are the Dane Women saying about those who go to war?

What is the 'ten-times-fingering weed' and what is it holding?

How does the man behave 'when the signs of summer thicken'?

What is the first (and last) verse saying about 'Woman'?

What is the **rhyme-scheme** *here?*

How many beats are there to a line? What is such a line called?

Abbey Tomb anthology pages 80–81

This is a **story** of a Viking raid, arising from an idea evoked by a tomb in an abbey.

What did the Vikings do?

Why did the inhabitants ring the bells?

Why did the speaker tell them not to?

The Vikings attacked very quickly: what three ideas are used in verse 3 to show this speed of attack?

In what way has the rain 'made their tombs look just as right as mine'?

What is the last verse saying about the passing of time?

The **rhyme-scheme** here is ABCB, but the rhymes here often involve the consonants rather than whole syllables, e.g. came/cream, hills/bells. The metre is **iambic** and the lines are alternately tetrameters and trimeters.

What is the rhyme-scheme here? Is there anything unusual about the rhymes?

Is there the same number of beats in each line?

Compare

Fighting South of the Castle V II:69
The Vote V II:69
Beaucourt Revisited NDBV:181

The War Song of Dinas Vawr anthology pages 82–83

This song comes from Peacock's novel *The Misfortunes of Elphin*, which is a parody of the Arthurian legends set in southern Wales, where Elphin is king of Caredigion. This story of plunder is told in a very matter-of-fact way – which is part of the parody, showing how easily accepted such killing was in such legends; and the pattern contributes to the apparent inevitability of the events.

(Words to explain: meeter – more suitable; carousing – drinking, celebrating; cravens – cowards)

Which sheep did they choose?

What was the sequence of events in this story of plunder and killing?

What is meant by 'The eagles and the ravens
We glutted with our foemen.'?

What is the difference between the two uses of 'head' in the last verse?

What did they sing about?

Plan a reading of this as a war-chant; then chant it in groups.

The rhyme-scheme and rhythm are very regular here, as is usual for a song or chant. The rhyme is ABAB and the rhythm is again iambic.

Compare:
The Destruction of Sennacherib *NDBV*:176

☐ **On the Late Massacre in Piedmont** anthology page 83

This poem conveys strongly the **feelings** aroused by merciless slaughter in the Easter massacre in Piedmont in 1655.

Piedmont is a region of north-west Italy bordering on France and Switzerland. A group of Protestant inhabitants had settled beyond permitted territorial limits and were evicted, on the orders of the Duke of Savoy, a Catholic prince, by an army under the Marquis of Pianezza. But the Marquis went further, stationed troops within the permitted boundaries and on April 24, 1655 laid waste the villages with fire and sword; the killing, together with the winter and hunger, took the lives of 1712 people. Some survivors got through the snowbound Alpine passes to tell their tale in Paris. Milton wrote this poem in May of the same year.

What has happened to the saints?

Why is the poem addressed 'O Lord'?

Who are being referred to in lines 3–4?

What is meant by 'their moans the vales redoubled to the hills and they to heaven'?

What does the poet hope will grow from the Italian fields?

Milton also writes this in an **iambic metre**, but these are pentameters while the War Song is in trimeters.

Try and show how these two poems are written in the same metre, but the second has more beats/feet to the line.

Compare:

The Charge of the Light Brigade NDBV:177

On the Massacre of Glencoe anthology pages 84–85

This **story** of treachery and massacre conveys the various moods and **feelings** of contempt and horror aroused by the famous Massacre of Glencoe in 1692. 120 governmental troops, led by a member of the Campbell clan, treacherously murdered 38 members of the Macdonald clan, the inhabitants of the glen, after they had lived for twelve days on friendly terms with the clansmen. The ground for this treachery was the failure of MacIan, chief of the Macdonald clan, to take the oath of allegiance by the appointed day.

The **pattern** and the rhythm help to bring out the relentlessness of the action.

This is a story of treachery: what exactly happened?

Where is the Harper playing and singing and what are his companions?

What point is being made in verse 2 about safety and security?

What details are given in verse 3 of the welcome given to the 'guests'?

What exactly is meant by 'the friendly hearth which warm'd the hand
At midnight arm'd it with the brand.'?

Why are the wind and snow mentioned in verse 5?

What is meant by the last half of verse 6?

The verses here divide into halves with the **rhyming** following a scheme of AAAB/CCCB. The rhythm is **iambic** and the lines are tetrameters.

Name the metre in which this is written and say how many feet there are to a line.

Compare, for its epic style:
Horatius NDBV:164

The New Dragon Book of Verse has a complete section on war.

Oh stay at home, my lad, and plough anthology page 85

The **feelings** expressed here, about going off to war rather than leading the home life, are simple but vivid: it echoes the sentiments of the Dane Women.

What is the lad being asked to do?

How is the idea of staying made attractive?

What is meant by 'plough the land and not the sea'?

Is this approach to war cowardly or sensible?

The Housman poem has a **rhyme-scheme** of ABCCB and is in **iambic** rhythm again.

How many beats are there to each line here? Is it the same number in each line?

How does the rhythm compare with that of the poem opposite?

Compare:

The Drum *V* II:73
The Dying Soldier *V* III:117
Anthem for Doomed Youth *NDBV*:183

□□ **Icarus Allsorts** anthology pages 86–87

This apparently light-hearted **story** has an undertone of irony and seriousness and shows the **feelings** of various groups of people towards disaster.

It will probably be necessary to explain that Icarus, in classical mythology, was the son of Daedalus, who fixed wings to his son's shoulders with wax as they both tried to escape from imprisonment. Icarus flew too near the sun, the wax melted and he fell into the sea and drowned.

When Roger McGough recorded this poem for the cassette he changed one or two words.

What are the main events of this story?

Why did the General press the button?

Why did he do it 'with glee and grinning'?

Why did bombs begin to fly 'from every corner of the earth'?

What were the 'mushrooms'?

Why do you think the rich were outside their fall-out shelters? And why like 'drunken carol singers'?

What is CND? Why should they scrawl 'I told you so'?

Why should the General have got the sack?

Is this in any way a serious poem?

Who was Icarus? Why is he included in the title?

Is this poem an example of **exaggeration** *or of* **understatement***?*

Is there any rhyme-scheme here? Is it at all regular?

Why do you think the poem is broken up the way it is? Does it contribute to its effect?

Compare:

Defence V III:130

Meeting at Night anthology page 88

The next five double-pages are of love poems, and hence deal primarily with the expression of **feelings**. This is a difficult subject to discuss with children, and the teacher should be satisfied that the class is capable of sensible, serious discussion. There are the additional problems of old-fashioned language and attitudes which we mentioned in the introduction.

In Meeting at Night *what does the poem describe?*

Why do the 'startled little waves' leap 'in fiery ringlets from their sleep'? Why 'fiery'?

How is the voice 'less loud' than the hearts?

In *Meeting at Night* the **rhyme scheme** is symmetrical but more complex: it is ABCCBA. The class might be asked to analyse the scheme and recognize this symmetry.

My mistress' eyes anthology page 89
☐ **The Prince of Love**

First poem:

Shakespeare here deliberately avoids the ideal features with which a girl might be compared: what comparisons is he suggesting other poets or lovers might make?

What does he really feel about his 'mistress'?

Shakespearean **sonnets** followed a **rhyme-scheme** of ABAB rhyme until the last two of the fourteen lines which were a rhyming couplet. The **iambic pentameter** is the favourite metre of Shakespeare in his poems and plays.

Compare the rhythm of this sonnet with that of A Dream *on page 90 and see how they are similar.*

Compare:

For Anne and *Song* *V* III:84
We'll Go No more A-Roving *V* III:85

Second poem:
Many poems express love as a **feeling** beyond one's control. This one uses the **image** of a captor to express the effect of love.

What does the prince of love represent?

What temptations does he offer the poet?

Where is love shown to have 'captured' the poet?

What creature is the poet represented as? What images support this?

Who is or was Phoebus?

How is love treating its captive in the last verse?

What is the **rhyme scheme**? *Is it regular?*
In what **metre** *is this written?*

Compare:

The Clod and the Pebble *V* III:97

A Dream anthology page 90
A Red, Red Rose anthology page 91

First poem:
In A Dream *what were the pigeons doing?*

Why were they 'too fond to fly'?

What happened to them?

Why should this dream be told to a lover? How could it relate to a pair of lovers?

Clare has a **rhyme-scheme** of ABAB in *First Love* on page 92 and the poem is in **iambic pentameters.**
The metre here is also iambic, but how many feet are there to a line?

Compare:
Strawberries V III:70
The Telephone V III:95

Second poem:
Burns expresses his **feelings** in terms of extremes, first with similes and then with comparisons with eternity.

Burns compares his love with three ideas: what are they?

He then says his love will last for ever: in what three ways does he express this eternity?

In A Red, Red Rose *the metre is* **iambic***: is each line metrically the same length?*

Compare:
How Much? V II:102
*She's Like the Swallow V III:*87

First Love anthology page 92

Clare here presents a detailed analysis of the **feelings** aroused by 'love at first sight'.

The poet is experiencing 'love at first sight': what different feelings does he describe?

What is meant by 'The trees and bushes round the place
Seemed midnight at noonday'?

What can he mean by 'Words from my eyes did start'?

How did the girl react to him?

How is the coldness of her response described?

First Love **rhymes** ABAB and is written in **iambic tetrameters** and is very regular.

Compare:

More *'Songs'* by Clare *V* II:106, 108
The Picnic *V* III:71
also *V* III:pages 82–3

Lines anthology page 93

Shelley echoes the **images** of winter and snow found in Clare's poem opposite.

The first two verses convey ideas of cold and dark: why does he start this way?
What contrasts are there in verse 3?
What is being described in verse 4?

The **rhyme-scheme** of *Lines* is more complex: ABCAAB. The metre is **iambic** and the beats/feet go 3:3:4:3:3. By keeping the same rhythm but increasing the length of the lines the words gather momentum as the reader progresses into the verse.

Compare:
Lovers in Winter V III:94

□ **The Passionate Shepherd to his Love** anthology page 94

This is the original poem, which has had its imitations and parodies: one is opposite. This original expresses all the simple prizes which a shepherd can offer his love. These prizes are the ideals in a pastoral life and thus convey his **feelings** strongly.

What is the shepherd offering to his love which is special to the countryside?

What is he offering which is special to a shepherd?

When do you think this poem was written?

Marlowe writes with a simple regular **rhyme-scheme** of couplets and in **iambic** metre.

Compare:

Elizabethan Sailor's Song V II:109
Then My Love and I'll Be Married V III:68

☐ **Come Live with Me** anthology page 95

This is an imitation of Marlowe, written by an Australian poet. It is obviously a parody, but it also expresses the same **feelings** in a different context.

The word 'lambent' means 'shining': what does 'when stars are lambing in the rivers' mean? Is there more than one meaning?

Why will they count the sheep 'by couples'?

In what way do 'hawks hang charmed above the plain'?

What are 'gallon hats'?

In what way is Time 'a shearer'? Do you know a similar representation of Time?

What do you think the 'super-bin' is?

Compare:

Sea Chest V III:88

To His Coy Mistress anthology pages 96–97

This well-known poem conveys the strength and urgency of **feelings** and the frustration aroused by coyness or 'playing hard-to-get'. Some of the imagery is adult, but the poem and its sentiments are appreciable by the young.

What do you understand by the word 'coy'?

What is the poet saying about the Lady's coyness in the first 20 lines?

In the second section what is meant by 'Time's winged chariot'? Why 'winged'? Why 'at my back'?

What are the 'deserts of vast eternity' and why are they before us?

What is 'thy marble vault'?

Why does he say 'The grave's a fine and private place
But none, I think, do there embrace.'?

Which two lines suggest the lovers should take their opportunities now and not be caught up by Time?

What do the last two lines say about Time?

Can you find two or three lines which sum up the whole poem?

Compare the rhyme-scheme and the metre here with that of The Passionate Shepherd.

Compare:
The Garden of Love V III:97

Evans anthology page 98

Evans is a poem outstanding in its sustained **images**. Note the rhetorical question at the beginning. This is a serious poem dealing with a dying man and may not therefore be suitable for general class discussion. There is a mixture of accurate, detailed description and compound metaphor.

Look at the first six lines and line 9. List five adjectives that give a depressing picture of the farm. Try saying the first verse with adjectives of opposite meaning.

Most of the rest of the poem is about two kinds of dark. What are they?

What is Evans being likened to in the last three and a half lines?

Which detail gives you the clearest picture of the farm or the dying man?

What are the writer's feelings about Evans?

What does R. S. Thomas use plain description for?

What does he describe in **metaphors***?*

What is the dominant metaphor?

List the words and phrases that sustain it.

Other deaths and old men:

Janet Waking (death of hen) *V* I:109
'Out, Out, –' *V* II:10
The Casualty *V* II:34
Death of a Whale (now possibly wrong) *V* II:53
The Dead Swagman *V* II:122
Bullocky (comparable dense imagery) *V* III:51
Beautify Old Age *V* III:56
It's Coming *V* III:103

Plastic Woman anthology page 99

After the deeply sympathetic *Evans*, *Plastic Woman* may seem rather slick and unsympathetic.

What does the lady have in her shopping bag?

Why is she described as a 'supermarket' shopping lady? (Is it only because she has been shopping in a supermarket?)

What could a 'dream booth' be?

Why is the operator described as 'Plastic'?

Why does the writer think the lady is 'Out of Order'?

In 'Plastic Woman' why are the lines divided as they are?

An opposite view:
Boy at the Window *V* I:125
She might reply:
Not Waving but Drowning *NDBV*:235

Upstream anthology pages 100–101

To appreciate *Upstream* you need to know that the Eskimo had no written language but everyone had his own laboriously composed songs. Its **images** lead to feelings of sadness and resignation.

What is there in the poem that tells you this is an old man talking?
What does he remember of his younger days?
Why is 'upstream' used at the end of so many verses?
Why does his song glide away from him?
In what way is making up a song or poem like fishing?

Other Eskimo songs:
The Old Man's Song *V* I:26
Magic Song *V* I:66
The Father's Song *V* I:129

The Astigmatic anthology page 102

This poem tells a story which evokes **feelings** of sympathy. It is written in a rather discursive 'unpoetic' style that contrasts sharply with *Who?* on the facing page. It has four sections:

1 his childhood experience
2 his present sight defect
3 associated problems
4 his dreams.

Why does he say the sun blew out?

Why does he say, 'screwing my tears into my work'?

Can you divide this poem into four different parts?

Which group of words gives the best idea of what it must be like to be so short-sighted?

What feelings does the last line give you?

With this you could read the Thurber short story, *The Admiral on the Wheel*, in *The Thurber Carnival* (Penguin).

A possible follow-up is:

My busconductor *V* III:50

Who? anthology page 103

Here is another strange way of seeing but the **images** are of the past, almost of ghosts.

Who is *that child?*

What gave you the clue?

At what point in the poem did you first think there was something strange about him?

Which line gives you the best picture of the past child?

Which of these two poems seems to you to be more 'poetic'?

Why do you think that?

Who? has a **rhyme-scheme** of ABCB and is written in a **dactylic** metre, the first and third lines as tetrameters, the second and fourth cut short in the fourth foot. The difference between the commoner iambic rhythm and dactylic can be brought out through this poem.

A similar mood is evoked in:

The Shepherd's Hut NDBV:213

Schoolmistress (Miss Humm) anthology page 105

The next two poems about school present a different world from that of today. Are the **feelings** the same? *Schoolmistress* contains many references that may need explaining. It is probably best to read the poem and then discuss the ones that cause problems. The whole poem is a good example of **hyperbole**.

Which picture of Miss Humm best suggests her authority?

Why were they no longer George or Tom or Mary?

What's strange about saying they halted in the 'middle' of a shout or a scream?

Why would it be so astonishing to think of her sleeping?

What was different about the Rector's voice compared with hers?

Do you think he exaggerates at all?

For these two pages:

Blue Umbrellas V III:156

A Boy's Head V III:167

and the school section of *NBDV*:113 to 119.

An Elementary School Classroom in a Slum anthology pages 106–107

It may be important to discuss social conditions forty years ago (1939) when this poem was written. The chapter on evacuees in *How We Lived Then* by Norman Longmate (Hutchinson, 1971) provides a good background. Even though standards of living have changed so dramatically, what Spender is saying may well still be true, and his **feelings** of anger still valid. It is probably best to read and discuss the first three verses of this difficult poem before tackling verse four.

What are the children like?

What is the view from the window?

What is the classroom decorated with?

What future have these children got?

Last verse: why do the windows 'open on their lives like crouching tombs'?

What might save these children from their doom?

□□ **You'd better believe him** anthology page 108

Before reading this poem it would be best to remind the class of what a fable is (Aesop's are the best known). This poem is a **story** with an implied moral. If you are reading it after the previous poem in the book you could link its moral to Spender's angry message.

'We have reason to believe him mad.' The last eight lines show that he wasn't, but such evidence isn't often available.

When Brian Patten recorded this poem for the cassette he changed one or two words.

What reasons do they have to believe him mad?

What reasons are there to suggest he isn't?

Fables often have morals. What might the moral of this one be?

The same writer's *Mr Moon's Last Case* is a novel dealing with the same situation.

See also:

Melody Grundy *V* I:25
O Taste and See *V* III:7
A Small Dragon *NDBV*:190
Snail of the Moon *NDBV*:192

Good Taste anthology page 109
There is no Frigate like a Book

First poem:
The detailed **images** are important in this story. It, too, has a moral.

What exactly happens in this poem?
Which details help you to imagine the scene?
What might the moral of this fable be?

The delicate **understatement** of the dangers in *Good Taste* fits the moral of the poem.

See also:
Blackberry Picking V II:10

Second poem:
Emily Dickinson's poem has four **images** to sum up the value of the imagination.

What four things is a book said to be like?
Why is poetry said to be 'prancing'?

Compare the **rhythm** and **rhyme** of this Emily Dickinson poem with her others in this book.

Compare the approach of:
On First Looking into Chapman's Homer NDBV:219

A Brown Paper Carrierbag anthology page 110

This poem deals with a distressing subject whose details we may prefer not to picture too closely. Its **images** are disturbing and it is probably best not to analyse them too closely (although they are well crafted) but to allow the feelings conveyed by the poem to make their own impact. It's possible to link this with *The Hangman at Home* (page 114).

It may be best not to use the following questions.

What is happening in this poem?

Where was the brown paperbag placed?

What feelings do you have when you read this poem?

What pattern does this poem have?

First Blood *V* II:38 deals with killing a squirrel.
A Poison Tree *V* II:86
Epitaph on a Tyrant *V* III:58
Five Ways to Kill a Man *NDBV*:220

New Members Welcome anthology page 111

New Members Welcome deals with the inside while the last poem dealt with the outside. Note how it uses negative **images**.

What is Spike Milligan saying about human beings?
Do you think it's true?
Which image do you like best?

See:
Courage V III:57

The Qualification anthology page 113

A humorous poem disguising strong **feelings**. Translated it reads:

work all your life
nothing to show
put on the news
same old drivel
    union bashing
    worker bashing
    Lord this
    Sir so-and-so that

Should hear my boy
Says we need guns
an armed revolution
nothing else works
    all right for him
    up at the uni(versity)
    Talk all you like there
    That's what it's for

Who is saying this?

What sort of man is he?

What do you know about his son?

Do you like the way this is written?

Read it aloud, following the spelling carefully.

Other dialect poems and related poems:

A Cockney Alphabet *V* I:16
Aunt's Tantrums VI:32
Abey! See de Gol'fish *V* I:79
How to Address a Bat, a Moth, a Dragon-Fly *V* I:100–101
False-Friends-Like *V* II:86
Counting *V* I:24
Epitaph on a 'Narf' *V* I:34
Keepen up o' Christmas *V* I:133

The Future anthology page 113

Another poem touching on the views of young and old. Its basic **image** is crucial for understanding the poem.

Was the old man really wise?

Why did the sides of the road converge?

This is really another fable. What is its moral?

In what way is this a poem?

Perhaps:

Five Ways to Kill a Man NDBV:220

The Hangman at Home anthology page 114

The next seven poems provide a macabre section on hanging and witches. They may provide an acceptable way of thinking about death and fear. This poem makes us think about the **feelings** of the hangman, or his lack of them, and, by extension, about our feelings about hanging.

What homely details are there in the poem?

What are these details being silently contrasted with?

Why shouldn't they look at his hands?

How might ordinary people react in the white face moon scene?

Why should everything be easy for a hangman?

What do you think are the writer's feelings about the hangman?

A Man of Words V I:13
The Gallows (NB animals) *V* I:74
The Sorrowful Lamentation V II:118
Cowboy Song V II:132
Lines Before Execution V II:149

On moonlit heath and lonesome bank anthology page 115

This poem has clear images and strong **feelings**.

Where is the speaker?
What is he waiting for?
Why are the sheep 'glimmering'?
Why do the trains 'groan' on the rail?
What are his feelings about the lad in Shrewsbury jail?
What detail gives you the clearest picture of the scene?

The Housman poem is in a regular pattern of ABAB **rhyme-scheme** and alternate **iambic** tetrameters/trimeters.

□ **Rizpah** anthology pages 116–119

Rizpah has been slightly shortened to save space. Depending on the class it might be best to summarize some of the **story** before reading the poem:

An old lady is dying and rambling in her mind, talking to a visitor who has come to sit by her. Her son Willy was hanged and she was so distressed that she was locked up as a lunatic. When she was let out only his bones were left on the gibbet. She took them one by one and buried them in the churchyard.

With a poem as long as this one, detailed discussions could become very tedious. It is probably best to deal only with problems that crop up and to practise and perform a reading.

What exactly happens in this story?

What are the mother's feelings?

Which lines give you the best picture of her desperation?

In groups practise a reading of this poem to bring out the best dramatic effect.

Rizpah is written in **rhyming couplets** and the lines have a break half-way through so that the beats are 3:3 to a line rather than six.

The Last Man V II:77
The Ballad of Charlotte Dymond V II:112
John Randall V II:133

Haunted anthology pages 120–121

This is an ambiguous poem. Is there really something after him, or is it his own **feelings** of guilt and fear?

What exactly happens in this poem?
Which lines make the wood sound unpleasant?
Which lines describe a pleasant contrast?
How do his feelings change as the poem goes on?
What did he die of?

The Nightmare V II:13
The Trap *NDBV*:210
Wuthering Heights *NDBV*:15
The Way through the Woods *NDBV*:18

Now the hungry lion roars anthology page 122
The Witches' Charm

These two poems deal with more traditional, and more distanced, fears. They both use **images** to create their effects.

First poem:
What mood does this poem produce in you?

How does it do this?

Which lines do you like best?

What does 'following darkness like a dream' mean?

Second poem:
Does this poem produce the same mood?

What sort of night is it?

These two poems contain some lively and varied use of rhythm and **rhyme**. The Shakespeare poem rhymes ABAB and is in **trochaic tetrameters**. *The Witches' Charm* rhymes ABCB and is in alternate **iambic tetrameters** and trimeters.

Other witches:
The Two Witches *V* I:51
Magic Song *V* I:66
The Hag *V* I:68
Witches' Song *NDBV*:193
and related:
The Cave of Despair *NDBV*:194

Pegasus anthology page 123

Pegasus links the world of witches back to the world of the rocking horse in Woolworths (p. 108). It is full of **images** whose cumulative effect is to create a living beast.

What is special about this horse?

Who can ride him?

How are his mane and forelock musical waves?

Why is love thought of as swift?

Which description of the horse do you like best?

Pegasus rhymes ABCB and the rhythm is **anapaestic**, running over in pairs of lines, e.g.

Hĭs whín|nў wăs swée|tĕr Thăn Órp|heŭs' lýre
Thĕ wíng|ŏn hĭs shóul|dĕr Wăs brígh|tĕr thăn fíre

For other magical horses see:
Horses on the Camargue *NDBV*:78

The Man in the Bowler Hat anthology page 124

After the macabre and fanciful, we end the book with two poems that deal with the ordinariness of people. The first could easily be seen as a gentle sneer, but is it?

What does the poet think about the man in the bowler hat?

What gives you the evidence for this?

What do you think about him?

Which lines suggest there is more to him than meets the casual eye?

What does the last line mean?

Follow-up poems:

I'm Nobody! Who are you? *V* I:26
A Civil Servant *V* II:123
As Others See Us *V* III:22
What is He *V* III:48
Mr Bleaney *NDBV*:145

Simplify me when I'm Dead anthology page 125

Keith Douglas is best known as a writer of the North African Campaign but was actually killed during the invasion of Normandy on June 9th, 1944 at the age of 24. This poem evokes a variety of **feelings** through its images.

What does 'simplify me' mean?

What are 'the processes of earth'?

Why do they leave him 'simpler than at birth'?

Look at verses 7 to 9 (Time's. . . . an opinion)

What will be the difference between an opinion about him arrived at ten years after his death and one immediately after?

Is there a paradox in the first two lines?

Poems that could be considered with this are:

I Am NDBV:233
And Death Shall have no Dominion NDBV:243
Afterwards NDBV:237

Index of titles and first lines

A littlebit of heaven fell 86
A thousand and fifty-one waves 71
A widow bird sate mourning for her love 29
Abbey Tomb 80
Advice to a Knight 16
After the first powerful plain manifesto 46
Against the rubber tongues of cows and the hoeing hands of men 56
Alone, in silence, at a certain time of night 47
Astigmatic, The 102
At seven the sun that lit my world blew out 102
At the old Ship Bank pub in Saltmarket 26
Avenge, O Lord, thy slaughtered saints, whose bones 83

Brown Paper Carrierbag, A 110

Carol of the Poor Children, The 41
Child on Top of a Greenhouse 33
Come, friendly bombs, and fall on Slough 64
Come live with me and be my love 94
Come live with me and we'll be drovers 95
Corner Seat 51

Daysies 34
Discovered an old rocking-horse in Woolworth's 108
Dog Lovers, The 72
Dream, A 90

Elementary School Class Room in a Slum, An 106
Epitaph in Lydford Churchyard 42
Epitaphs, short 8
Evans? Yes, many a time 98
Evening was in the wood, louring with storm 120
Express, The 46

Far far from gusty waves, these children's faces 106
Fear of flowers, The 52
Fetching Cows 30
First Love 92
Fog, The 38
Forlorn Sea, The 14
Friday Morning 40
From the blood of Medusa 123
Future, The 113

Galloping Cat, The 24
Glasgow October 1972 26
Good taste 109
Goody Blake and Harry Gill 18

Had we but world enough and time 96
Half grown before half seen 57
Hammers, The 63
Hangman at Home, The 114
Harp Song of the Dane Women 79
Haunted 120
Here is the News 12
Here lies a poor woman who always was tired 45
Here lies in a horizontal position the outside case of 42
How sweet I roamed from field to field 89

I am the unnoticed, the unnoticeable man 124
I had a dove 70
In Manchester today a man was seen 12
I ne'er was struck before that hour 92
I often go back 100
I saw the fog grow thick 38
I told them not to ring the bells 80
I went to the doctor, yes 10
Icarus Allsorts 86
I'm by nature solitary 17
In the third-class seat sat the journeying boy 50
In the time . . . 110
Inscription by the Sea, An 45
It was on a Friday morning that they took me from the cell 40

Lily, The 36
Limericks 6
Lines 93
Local Train of Thought, A 47

Man in the Bowler Hat, The 124
Meeting at Night 88
Midnight on the Great Western 50
Milk for the Cat 27
Mist in the Meadows 37
My love is like a red, red rose 91
My mistress' eyes are nothing like the sun 89
My mother saw a Dancing Bear 73

New Members Welcome 111
No dust have I to cover me 45
Noise of hammers once I heard 63
November Night, Edinburgh 39
Now have I thereto this condicioun 34
Now the hungry lion roars 122

Number 14 63
Numbers 71
'O tell me, Harper, wherefore flow 84
O why do you walk through the fields in gloves 51
Oh I am a cat that likes to 24
Oh stay at home, my lad, and plough 85
Oh! what's the matter? what's the matter 18
Old English Riddle 17
On moonlit heath and lonesome bank 115
On the Late Massacre in Piedmont 83
On the Massacre of Glencoe 84
Once at Piertarvit 68
Once in a dream (for once I dreamed of you) 90
One summer evening (led by her) I found 76
Our Princess married 14

Passionate Shepherd to his Love, The 94
Pegasus 123
Plastic Woman 99
Prelude, from The 76
Prince of Love, The 89
Pull the blinds 111
Pylons, The 67

Qualification, The 113

Red, Red Rose, A 91
Remember me when I am dead 125
Requiem 45
Rizpah 116

Saturdays I put on my boots to go wading 22
Schoolmistress 105
Silver against blue sky 53
Simplify me when I'm Dead 125
Slough 64
So they bought you 72
Song 43
Song (Keats) 70
Song of the Battery Hen 74
Spiritual Railway, The 44
Stanzas 78
Straightbacked as a Windsor chair 105
Stranger, approach this spot with gravity 9
Suspended in a moving night 51

Telegraph Poles 66
That house you took me to 63
The black one, last as usual, swings her head 30
The cold earth slept below 93
The Dandelion's pallid tube 37
The evening o'er the meadows seems to stoop 37
The fog comes 39
The grey sea and the long black land 88
The line to heaven by Christ was made 44
The modest rose puts forth a thorn 36
The mountain sheep are sweeter 82
The night tinkles like ice in glasses 39
The nodding oxeye bends before the wind 52
The owl is abroad, the bat, and the toad 122
The secret of these hills was stone, and cottages 67
The Spider holds a Silver Ball 31
The wind began to rock the Grass 32
The wind billowing out the seat of my britches 33
The young boy stood looking up the road 113
There is no Frigate like a Book 109
There was a young man of Bengal 6
These, in the dusk, are bars 66
Think of this tower-block 59
Thistle (Lee) 54
Thistles (Hughes) 56
Thistles (Stallworthy) 57
Thistle, blue bunch of daggers 54
Thistledown 53
To a Fat Lady Seen from the Train 51
To His Coy Mistress 96
Travelling, a man met a tiger, so . . . 109
Tremors 48

Under the wide and starry sky 45
Upstream 100

Wailing, wailing, wailing, the wind over land and sea 116
War Song of Dinas Vawr, The 82
We are the poor children, come out to see the sights 41
We can't grumble about accommodation 74
We took turns at laying 48
Wear modest armour; and walk quietly 16
What are you saying 99
What does the hangman think about 114
What is a woman that you forsake her 79
When a man hath no freedom to fight for at home 78
When I am dead my dearest 43
When the tea is brought at five o'clock 27
Who is that child I see wandering, wandering 103
Widow Bird, A 29
Witches' Charm, The 122
wurk air yir life 113

You'd better believe him 108

Index of authors

BEER, Patricia (1924–) 80
BETJEMAN, John (1906–) 64
BLAKE, William (1757–1827) 36
BOSLEY, Keith (1937–) 63
BROCK, Edwin (1927–) 74
BROWNING, Robert (1812–1889) 88
BURNS, Robert (1759–1796) 91
BYRON, Lord George (1788–1824) 78
CAMPBELL, David (1915–) 95
CARTER, Sydney (1915–) 40
CAUSLEY, Charles (1917–) 73, 103
CHAUCER, Geoffrey (?1340–1400) 34
CLARE, John (1793–1864) 52, 92, 37
CONN, Stewart (1936–) 48
CORNFORD, Frances (1886–1960) 49
DAVIES, W. H. (1871–1940) 38
DEHN, Paul (1912–) 66
DICKINSON, Emily (1830–1886) 37, 109, 31, 32
DOUGLAS, Keith (1920–1944) 125
FARJEON, Eleanor (1881–1965) 123
HARDY, Thomas (1840–1928) 50
HOBSBAUM, Philip (1932–) 102
HODGSON, Ralph (1871–1962) 63
HOUSMAN, A. E. (1859–1936) 85, 115
HUGHES, Ted (1930–) 56
IKINILIK 100
JONES, T. H. (1921–1965) 16
JONSON, Ben (1573–1637) 122
KEATS, John (1795–1821) 70
KIPLING, Rudyard (1865–1936) 79
LEE, Laurie (1914–) 54
LOGUE, Christopher (1926–) 109
LEONARD, Tom (1944–) 113
MacCAIG, Norman (1910–) 30, 39
McGOUGH, Roger (1937–) 110, 86
MacNEICE, Louis (1907–1963) 51
MARLOWE, Christopher (1564–1593) 94
MARVELL, Andrew (1621–1678) 96
MIDDLETON, Richard (1882–1911) 41
MILLIGAN, Spike (1919–) 72, 111, 99, 113
MILTON, John (1608–1674) 83
MONRO, Harold (1879–1932) 27
MORGAN, Edwin (1920–) 26
PATTEN, Brian (1946–) 108
PEACOCK, Thomas Love (1785–1866) 82
REID, Alastair (1926–) 68
ROETHKE, Theodore (1908–1963) 33
ROSEN, Michael (1946–) 12, 10, 22, 59
ROSSETTI, Christina (1830–1894) 90, 43
SANDBURGH, Carl (1878–1967) 39, 114
SANSOM, Clive (1910–) 105
SASSOON, Siegfried (1886–1967) 120, 47
SCOTT, Sir Walter (1771–1832) 84
SHAKESPEARE, William (1564–1616) 89, 122
SHELLEY, Percy Bysshe (1792–1822) 29, 93
SMITH, Stevie (1902–1971) 14, 24, 71
SPENDER, Stephen (1909–) 106, 46, 67
STALLWORTHY, Jon (1935–) 57
STEVENSON, Robert Louis (1850–1894) 45
TENNYSON, Alfred Lord (1809–1892) 116
TESSIMOND, A. S. J. (1902–1962) 124
THOMAS, R. S. (1913–) 98
WORDSWORTH, William (1770–1850) 18, 76
YOUNG, Andrew (1885–1971) 53

Acknowledgements

The editors and publisher acknowledge permission to use the following copyright poems:

Patricia Beer: 'Abbey Tomb' from *Just Like The Resurrection* (Macmillan). Reprinted by permission of the author. **John Betjeman:** 'Slough' from *Collected Poems.* Reprinted by permission of John Murray (Publishers) Ltd. **Keith Bosley:** 'Number 14' (copyright © 1979 Keith Bosley) from *Young British Poets* (Chatto). Reprinted by permission of the author. **Edwin Brock:** 'Song of the Battery Hen' from *Song of the Battery Hen* (Secker & Warburg). Reprinted by permission of David Higham Associates Ltd. **David Campbell:** 'Come Live With Me and We'll be Drovers' from *Selected Poems.* Reprinted by permission of the author's literary estate and Angus & Robertson (UK) Ltd. **Sydney Carter:** 'Friday Morning' from *Greenprint for Song.* Reprinted by permission of Stainer & Bell Ltd. **Charles Causley:** 'My Mother Saw a Dancing Bear' from *Collected Poems* and 'Who' from *Figgie Hobbin* (both Macmillan). Reprinted by permission of David Higham Associates Ltd. **Stewart Conn:** 'Tremors' from *Ear To The Ground.* Reprinted by permission of Hutchinson Publ. Group Ltd. **Frances Cornford:** 'To a Fat Lady Seen from the Train' from *Collected Poems* (Barrie & Jenkins). Reprinted by permission of Hutchinson Publ. Group Ltd. **W. H. Davies:** 'The Fog' from *The Complete Poems of W. H. Davies.* Reprinted by permission of the Executors of the W. H. Davies Estate and Jonathan Cape Ltd. **Paul Dehn:** 'Telegraph Poles' from *The Fern on The Rock* (copyright © Dehn Enterprises Ltd., 1965, 1976). Reprinted by permission of Hamish Hamilton, London. **Keith Douglas:** 'Simplify Me When I'm Dead' from *The Complete Poems of Keith Douglas* (edited by Desmond Graham 1978). Reprinted by permission of Oxford University Press. **Eleanor Farjeon:** 'Pegasus' from *Collected Poems* Michael Joseph Ltd). Reprinted by permission of David Higham Associates Ltd. **Philip Hobsbaum:** 'The Astigmatic' from *In Retreat* (Macmillan). Reprinted by permission of the author. **Ralph Hodgson:** 'The Hammers' from *Collected Poems.* Reprinted by permission of Mrs. Hodgson and Macmillan, London and Basingstoke. **A. E. Housman:** 'Oh, stay at home . . .' and 'On moonlit heath . . .' (Poems XXXVIII and IX) from *Collected Poems* (Cape). Reprinted by permission of The Society of Authors as the literary representatives of the Estate of A. E. Housman. **Ted Hughes:** 'Thistles' from *Wodwo.* Reprinted by permission of Faber & Faber Ltd. **Ikinilik:** 'Upstream' from *Eskimo Poems From Canada and Greenland* (translated by Tom Lowenstein). Reprinted by permission of Allison & Busby Ltd. **T. H. Jones:** 'Advice to a Knight' from *The Colour of Cockcrowing.* Reprinted by permission of Granada Publishing Ltd. **Laurie Lee:** 'Thistle' from *The Bloom of Candles* (Hogarth Press). Reprinted by permission of the author. **Tom Leonard:** 'The Qualification' from *Bunnit Husslin* (Third Eye Centre, Glasgow). Reprinted by permission of the author. **C. Logue:** 'Good Taste' from *Songs* (Hutchinson). Reprinted by permission of Hope Leresche & Sayle. **Norman MacCaig:** 'Fetching Cows' from *Measures.* Reprinted by permission of Chatto & Windus Ltd. 'November Night, Edinburgh' from *The Sinai Sort.* Reprinted by permission of The Hogarth Press Ltd. **Roger McGough:** 'Icarus Allsorts' (copyright © 1967 by Roger McGough) from *Penguin Modern Poets 10*, and 'A Brown Paper Bag' (copyright © 1976 by Roger McGough) from *In The Classroom* (Cape). Both reprinted by permission of Hope Leresche and Sayle. **Spike Milligan:** 'The Dog Lovers', 'Plastic Woman', 'New Members Welcome' and 'The Future', all from *Small Dreams of a Scorpion.* Reprinted by permission of Michael Joseph Ltd. **Harold Monro:** 'Milk for the cat' from *Collected Poems.* Reprinted by permission of Gerald Duckworth & Co. Ltd. **Edwin Morgan:** 'Glasgow October 1972' from *A Sense of Belonging* (Blackie). Reprinted by permission of the author. **Brian Patten:** 'You'd better believe him' from *Notes to the Hurrying Man.* Reprinted by permission of George Allen & Unwin Ltd. **Alistair Reid:** 'Once at Piertarvit' from *Oddments, Inklings, Omens, Moments* (Little, Brown & Co.). Reprinted by permission of Laurence Pollinger Ltd. **Edwin Arlington Robinson:** 'An Inscription by the Sea' ('Variations of Greek Themes', XI), from *Collected Poems* (copyright 1915 by Edwin Arlington Robinson, renewed 1943 by Ruth Nivison). Reprinted by permission of Macmillan Publishing Co., Inc. **Theodore Roethke:** 'Child on top of a greenhouse' from *The Collected Poems of Theodore Roethke.* Reprinted by permission of Faber & Faber Ltd. **Michael Rosen:** 'Think of this tower block', 'I Went to the Doctor' and 'Here is the News' all from *Wouldn't You Like to Know.* 'Saturdays I put my boots on' from *Mind Your Own Business.* All reprinted by permission of André Deutsch Ltd. **Carl Sandburg:** 'Fog' from *Chicago Poems* (copyright 1916 by Holt, Rinehart and Winston, Inc.; copyright 1944 by Carl Sandburg). 'The Hangman at Home' from *Smoke and Steel* (copyright by permission of Harcourt Brace Jovanovich, Inc. **Clive Sansom:** 'Schoolmistress (Miss Humm)' from *Dorset Village* (Methuen). Reprinted by permission of David Higham Associates Ltd. **Siegfried Sassoon:** 'A Local Train of Thought' and 'Haunted' from *Collected Poems* (Faber). Both reprinted by permission of George T. Sassoon. **Stevie Smith:** 'The Forlorn Sea', 'The Galloping Cat' and 'Numbers' all from *The Collected Poems of Stevie Smith* (Allen Lane). Reprinted by permission of James MacGibbon as executor. **Stephen Spender:** 'The Express', 'The Pylons' and 'An Elementary School Classroom in a Slum', all from *Collected Poems.* Reprinted by permission of Faber & Faber Ltd. **Jon Stallworthy:** 'Thistles' from *Root and Branch.* Reprinted by permission of Chatto & Windus Ltd. **A. S. J. Tessimond:** 'The Man in the Bowler Hat' from *Not Love Perhaps* (Autolyous Press). Reprinted by permission of Hubert Nicolson as literary executor to ASJ Tessimond. **R. S. Thomas:** 'Evans' from *Selected Poems 1946–1968.* Reprinted by permission of Granada Publishing Ltd. **Andrew Young:** 'Thistledown' from *Complete Poems* (edited by Leonard Clark). Reprinted by permission of Martin Secker & Warburg Ltd.